ADULT ALL-IN-ONE COURSE

LESSON · THEORY · TECHNIC

P9-DCZ-475

FOREWORD

Alfred's Basic Adult All-in-One Course, Level 1, is designed for the beginner looking for a truly complete piano course that includes lesson, theory, technic and popular repertoire in one convenient, all-in-one book. This course has a number of features that make it particularly successful in achieving this goal.

1. It progresses very smoothly, leaving no gaps that might cause the student to skip difficult sections.

2. Because it teaches chord-playing in both hands, songs are more musical, and playing becomes a richer, more rewarding experience.

3. Also taught is the understanding of how chords are formed. Instead of memorizing chords, students learn how to derive them regardless of what key they are playing in.

4. The choice of song material is outstanding, with some popular and familiar favorites mixed with tuneful originals, all adding to the fun and enjoyment of making music.

5. For the first time, an adult course has combined Lesson, Theory and Technic sections within one book. This combined approach offers beginners a unified course of instruction.

    A. **Lesson pages** are designed to provide a basic course of instruction that contains all the concepts and fundamentals needed to perform.

    B. **Theory pages** give beginners an added understanding of music which cannot be taught any other way. Every concept and principle introduced in the Lesson pages is reinforced. Additional drills in note recognition make this a valuable aid in developing reading skills. Important tips are presented that make learning chord progressions easier.

    C. **Technic pages** offer suggestions for the proper care of your hands. Most adult beginners feel awkward at the keyboard because of stiffness in their fingers, hands and wrists. They have trouble with coordination, and they feel they could play much better if the muscular agility and flexibility of their hands could somehow be made to keep pace with their comprehension. The Technic pages included have been developed to make all this possible.

At the completion of this course, the student will have learned to play some of the most popular music ever written and will have gained a thorough understanding of the basic concepts of music. The student will then be ready to begin Alfred's Basic Adult All-in-One Course, Level 2 (#14514).

Willard A. Palmer
Morton Manus
Amanda Vick Lethco

A General MIDI disk (5725) and CD (11282) are available, both of which offer a full piano recording and background accompaniment.

ISBN 0-88284-818-6
ISBN 978-0-88284-818-1

Cover photo: Jeff Oshiro

Contents

Preliminary Exercises

BE KIND TO YOUR HANDS!

No part of the body takes more abuse than the hands. We wear shoes on our feet to protect them against the rough surfaces they walk on. Our hands are almost constantly exposed to the elements and to the rough things we do to them. Gloves are usually worn only to keep the hands warm in cold weather.

If you want to keep your hands in playing condition, it is best to wear gloves when you are lifting large, heavy objects, as well as when you are working with tools such as screwdrivers, pliers, wrenches, spades and pruning shears.

USE A LITTLE WARM WATER

Before practicing, it is good to soak the hands for a few minutes in warm water. This promotes circulation. Many concert pianists use very warm water on their hands before beginning to play. Towel the hands vigorously until they are dry, then hold your arms out with the hands dangling from the wrist, and shake out your hands rapidly for a few moments.

DANGLE FROM
WRISTS

SHAKE OUT
HANDS

No. 1   **a)** Holding your arms in playing position, palms downward, clench both hands tightly, making two fists. Hold while you count "ONE–TWO."

MAKE TIGHT
FISTS

PALMS
DOWN

b) SNAP the fingers quickly outward, opening both hands. Do this with great vigor. Hold this position with all fingers extended. Count "THREE–FOUR."

SNAP FINGERS
OPEN

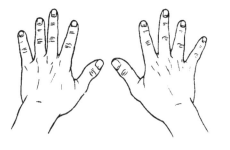

PALMS
DOWN

c) Shake out both hands, dangling from the wrists. Count "ONE–TWO–THREE–FOUR."

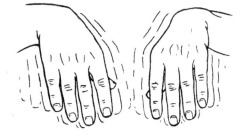

No. 2 **a)** Repeat the beginning of the previous exercise, with PALMS UPWARD. Clench both hands, making two fists. Hold and count "ONE–TWO."

MAKE TIGHT
FISTS

PALMS
UP

b) SNAP the fingers outward (palms up), opening both hands. Hold fingers outward as you count "THREE–FOUR."

SNAP FINGERS
OPEN

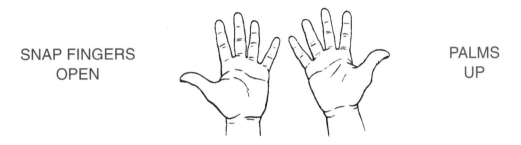

PALMS
UP

c) Turn hands over, palms down, hands dangling from the wrists, and shake out. Count "ONE–TWO–THREE–FOUR."

DANGLE FROM
WRISTS

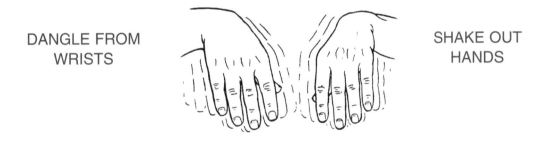

SHAKE OUT
HANDS

No. 3   Combining DEEP-BREATHING with Preliminary Exercise No. 1

Seated at the piano, repeat step **a)** of Preliminary Exercise No. 1, clenching the fists with palms downward, while breathing IN (the lower abdomen moves outward). Mentally count "ONE–TWO."

Repeat step **b)**, snapping the fingers outward, expelling the air while mentally counting "THREE–FOUR."

Repeat step **c)**, shaking out your hands as you inhale, mentally counting "ONE–TWO–THREE–FOUR." Continue as you exhale, counting "ONE–TWO–THREE–FOUR."

To avoid possible dizziness due to hyperventilation, this exercise should not be repeated more than two or three times at first.

No. 4   Combining DEEP-BREATHING with Preliminary Exercise No. 2

Follow the procedure described just above, clenching the hands and snapping the fingers outward with PALMS UP. Turn hands over, palms down, hands dangling from the wrists, and shake out.

How to Sit at the Piano

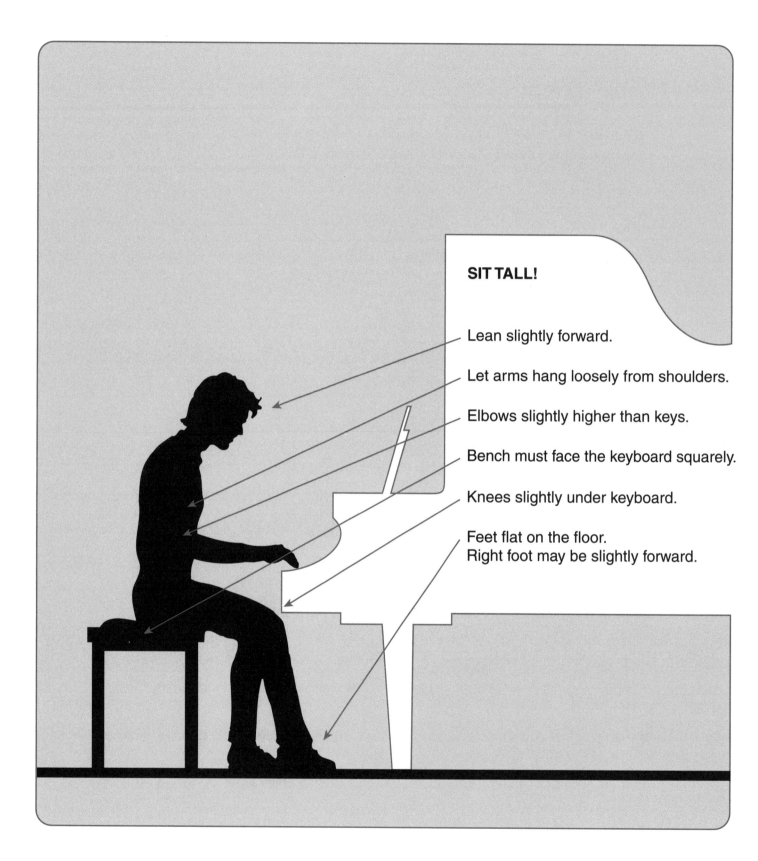

SIT TALL!

Lean slightly forward.

Let arms hang loosely from shoulders.

Elbows slightly higher than keys.

Bench must face the keyboard squarely.

Knees slightly under keyboard.

Feet flat on the floor.
Right foot may be slightly forward.

Finger Numbers

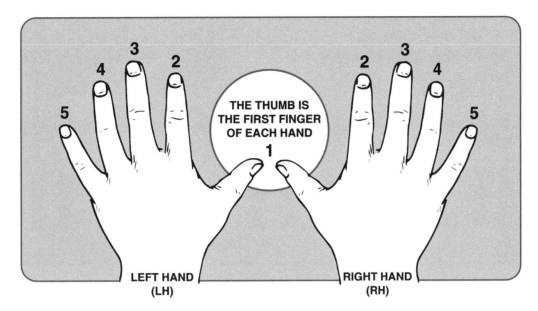

LEFT HAND
(LH)

RIGHT HAND
(RH)

THE THUMB IS
THE FIRST FINGER
OF EACH HAND

Response to reading finger numbers should be automatic. Before you begin to play, practice moving each finger as you say its number aloud.

Piano Tones

When you play a key, a hammer inside your piano touches a string to make a tone.

When you drop into a key with a LITTLE weight, you make a SOFT tone.

When you use MORE weight, you make a LOUDER tone.

String

Hammer

Curve your fingers when you play!

Pretend you have a bubble in your hand.

Hold the bubble gently, so it doesn't break!

1. Play any white key with the 3rd finger of either hand, softly.

2. See how many times you can repeat the same key, making each tone a little louder.

Before you play any key, you should always decide how soft or loud you want it to sound.

For the first pieces in this book, play with a MODERATELY LOUD tone.

The Keyboard

The keyboard is made up of white keys and black keys.
The black keys are in groups of twos and threes.

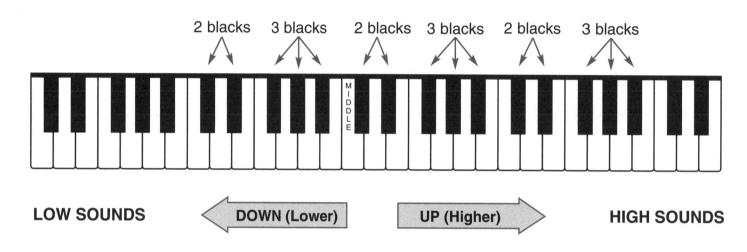

On the keyboard, DOWN is to the LEFT, and UP is to the RIGHT.
As you move LEFT, the tones sound LOWER. As you move RIGHT, the tones sound HIGHER.

Play the 2-BLACK-KEY groups!

LH

1. Using LH 2 3, begin at the middle and play all the 2-black-key groups going DOWN the keyboard (both keys at once).

2. Using RH 2 3, begin at the middle and play all the 2-black-key groups going UP the keyboard (both keys at once).

RH

Play the 3-BLACK-KEY groups!

LH

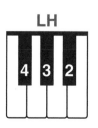

3. Using LH 2 3 4, begin at the middle and play all the 3-black-key groups going DOWN the keyboard (all three keys at once).

4. Using RH 2 3 4, begin at the middle and play all the 3-black-key groups going UP the keyboard (all three keys at once).

RH

Name That Key!

Piano keys are named for the first seven letters of the alphabet, beginning with **A.**

A B C D E F G

Each white key is recognized by its position in or next to a black-key group!
For example: **A**'s are found between the **TOP TWO KEYS** of each **3-BLACK-KEY GROUP.**

Play the following.   Use LH 3 for keys below the middle of the keyboard.
　　　　　　　　　　Use RH 3 for keys above the middle of the keyboard.
　　　　　　　　　　Say the name of each key aloud as you play!

Play all the **A**'s
on your piano.

Play all the **B**'s.

Play all the **C**'s.

Play all the **D**'s.

Play all the **E**'s.

Play all the **F**'s.

Play all the **G**'s.

You can now name every white key on your piano!
The key names are **A B C D E F G**, used over and over!

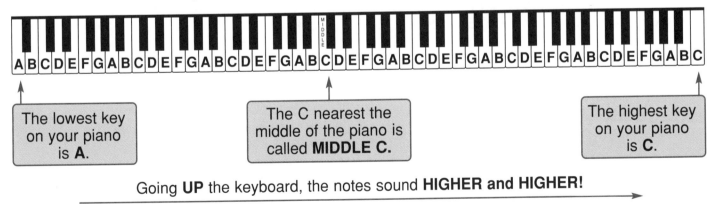

The lowest key
on your piano
is **A.**

The C nearest the
middle of the piano is
called **MIDDLE C.**

The highest key
on your piano
is **C.**

Going **UP** the keyboard, the notes sound **HIGHER and HIGHER!**

Play and name every white key beginning with bottom A.
Use LH 3 for keys below middle C, and RH 3 for keys above middle C.

Isometric Exercise

An isometric exercise is one in which one set of muscles is briefly tensed in opposition to another set of muscles, or in opposition to a solid surface.

To prepare for this exercise, press the hands flatly together with all fingers touching, in a "prayer position."

Now slowly bring the palms apart, with fingertips touching, until all fingers are in a curved position.

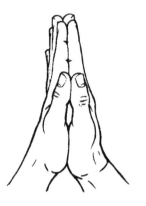

EXERCISE: Keep fingers in the curved position, relaxed.

Now press the 3rd fingers firmly together. Keep the other fingers relaxed. Do this four times, counting "ONE–TWO–THREE–FOUR."

Do the same with the 2nd fingers, then the 4th fingers, then the thumbs, and finally with the 5th fingers.

Repeat several times, then shake out your hands vigorously. Repeat again.

A Beneficial Hand Massage

1. Place the back of the left hand in the palm of the right hand, relaxed and flat.
2. With the thumb of the right hand, massage the left hand along the ridge of the fingers and along the fleshy part of the base of the thumb. Do not use excessive pressure, or you may bruise the hand. Continue this for about 30 seconds.

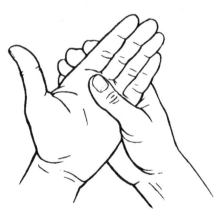

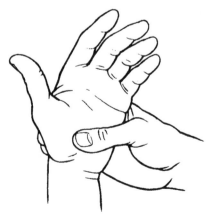

3. Reverse hands, massaging the right hand with the left.
4. Shake out the hands vigorously for several seconds.

This exercise should be beneficial to circulation and should make the hands more flexible.

Four Good Reasons for Playing with Curved Fingers

1. When the fingers are straight, each finger has a different length.

When the fingers are curved, each finger has, in effect, the same length.

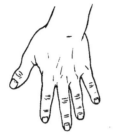

2. If your fingers are straight, the thumb cannot be properly used.

Curved fingers bring the thumb into the correct playing position.

3. Straight fingers will bend at the first joint, opposite to the motion of the key, delaying key response.

With curved fingers, keys respond instantly. You are IN CONTROL when you CURVE!

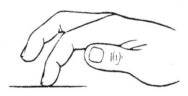

4. Moving over the keys will require turning the thumb *under* the fingers and crossing fingers *over* the thumb. Curved fingers provide an ARCH that makes this motion possible.

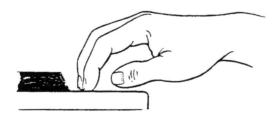

VERY IMPORTANT! Keep fingernails reasonably SHORT. It is impossible to curve fingers properly with long fingernails.

Right Hand C Position

Place the RH on the keyboard so that the **1st FINGER** falls on **MIDDLE C.**
Let the remaining 4 fingers fall naturally on the next 4 white keys.
Keep the fingers curved and relaxed.

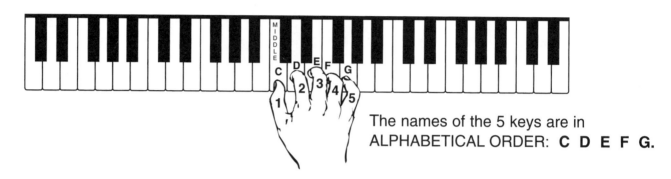

The names of the 5 keys are in
ALPHABETICAL ORDER: **C D E F G.**

Notes for this position are written on the TREBLE STAFF.

The TREBLE STAFF has 5 lines and 4 spaces.

Middle C is written on a short line
below the staff, called a *leger* line.

TREBLE CLEF SIGN:
used for RH notes.

D is written in the space below the staff.

Each next higher note is written
on the next higher line or space.

Fingering:

RIGHT HAND WARM-UP 🔊 *

Play the following *WARM-UP.* Say the name of each note aloud as you play.
Repeat until you can play smoothly and evenly. As the notes go higher on the keyboard,
they are written higher on the staff!

* 🔊 This symbol indicates the track number of the selection on the CD. See the General MIDI (GM) disk
  sleeve for the GM track numbers.

Quarter Notes & Half Notes

Music is made up of **short** tones and **long** tones. We write these tones in **notes,** and we measure their lengths by **counting**. The combining of notes into patterns is called RHYTHM.

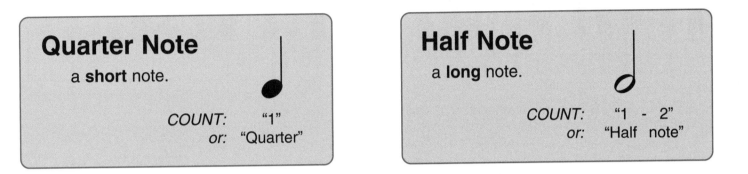

Quarter Note

a **short** note.

COUNT: "1"
or: "Quarter"

Half Note

a **long** note.

COUNT: "1 - 2"
or: "Half note"

Clap (or tap) the following rhythm. Clap ONCE for each note, counting aloud.

Notice how the BAR LINES divide the music into MEASURES of equal duration.

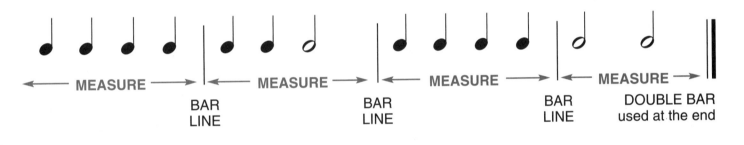

ODE TO JOY *(Theme from Beethoven's 9th Symphony)*

1. Clap (or tap) the rhythm evenly, counting aloud.

2. Play & sing (or say) the finger numbers.

3. Play & count.

4. Play & sing (or say) the note names.

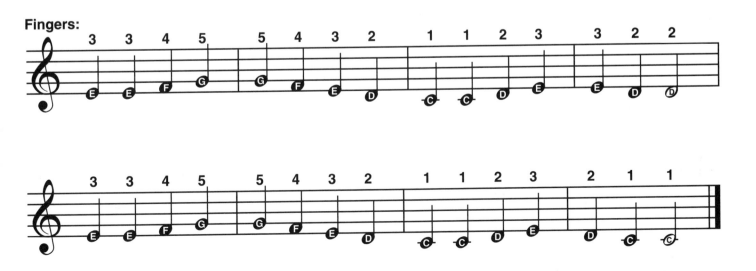

The Treble Clef Sign

locates the **G** above the middle of the keyboard.

This sign came from the letter **G**:

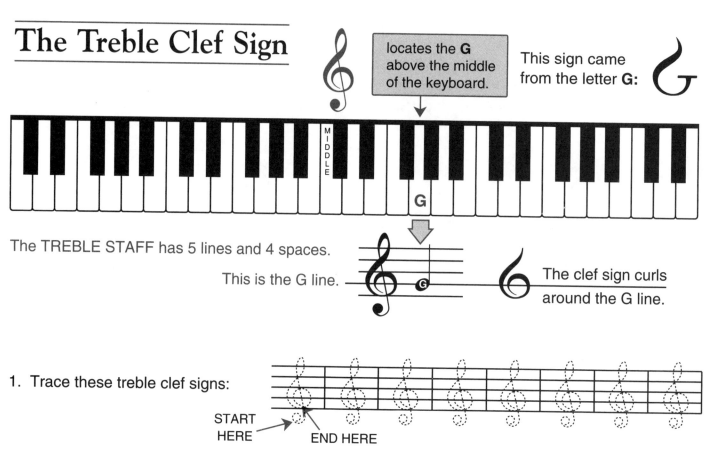

The TREBLE STAFF has 5 lines and 4 spaces.

This is the G line.

The clef sign curls around the G line.

1. Trace these treble clef signs:

   START HERE → ← END HERE

2. Draw a line of treble clef signs.

REVIEW

The notes of the RIGHT HAND **C POSITION** are written on the **TREBLE STAFF.**

- Middle C is written on a short line below the staff, called a *leger* line.

- D is written in the space below the staff.

- Each next higher note is written on the next higher line or space.

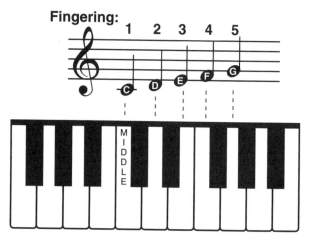

Fingering: 1 2 3 4 5

3. Write the names of the 5 notes in RH C position on the keyboard to the right.

4. Write the name of each note in the box below it.

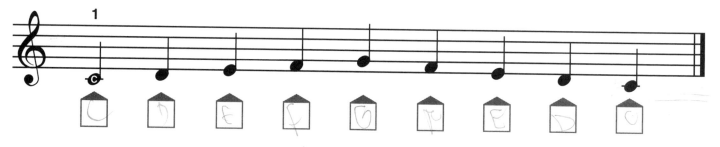

5. These notes are on LINES. Write the name of each note in the box below it.

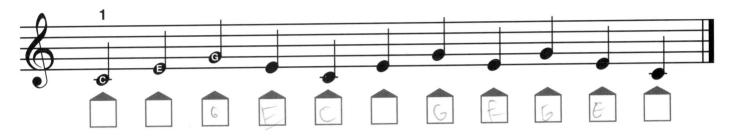

| | | G | E | C | | G | F | G | E | |

6. These notes are in SPACES. Write the name of each note in the box below.

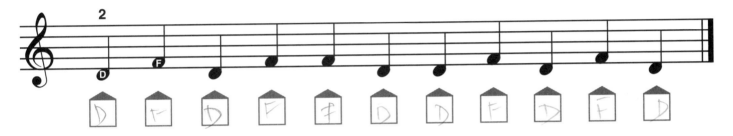

| D | F | D | F | F | D | D | F | D | F | D |

7. Here are notes on LINES & SPACES. Write the name of each note in the box.

| C | E | D | F | E | B | E | F | D | E | C |

| G | E | F | D | E | C | E | D | F | E | G |

8. When a note repeats on the SAME line or space, the note is repeated on the keyboard.
Write the name of each note in the box below it.

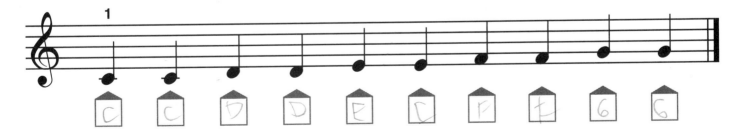

| C | C | D | D | E | E | F | F | G | G |

9. Above each note on this page, write the finger number used to play it in RH C POSITION.

10. Play all the notes on this page in RH C POSITION.

Left Hand C Position

Place the LH on the keyboard so that the **5th FINGER** falls on the **C BELOW** (to the left of) **MIDDLE C.**
Let the remaining fingers fall naturally on the next 4 white keys.
Keep the fingers curved and relaxed.

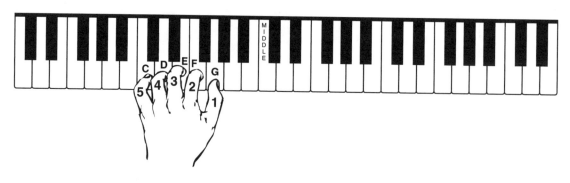

Notes for this position are written on the BASS STAFF.

The BASS STAFF also has
5 lines and 4 spaces.

The C, played by 5,
is written on the
second space of the staff.

Each next higher note is written
on the next higher line or space.

BASS CLEF SIGN:
used for LH notes.

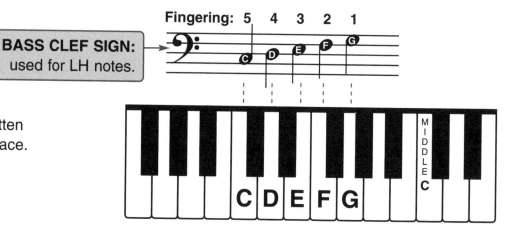

LEFT HAND WARM-UP

Play the following *WARM-UP.* Say the name of each note aloud as you play.
Repeat until you can play smoothly and evenly.

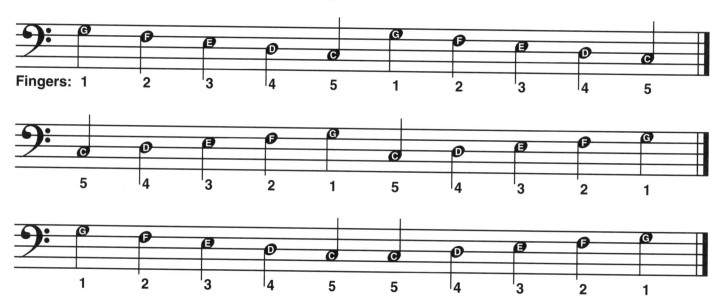

When notes are BELOW the MIDDLE LINE of the staff, the stems usually point UP.
When notes are ON or ABOVE the MIDDLE LINE, the stems usually point DOWN.

The Whole Note

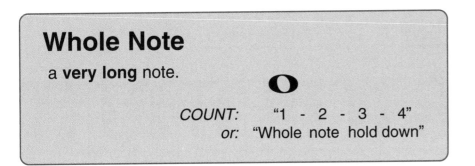

Whole Note

a **very long** note.

COUNT: "1 - 2 - 3 - 4"
or: "Whole note hold down"

Clap (or tap) the following rhythm. Clap ONCE for each note, counting aloud.

AURA LEE 🔊

This melody was made into a popular song, "Love Me Tender," sung by Elvis Presley.

1. Clap (or tap) the rhythm, counting aloud.

2. Play & sing (or say) the finger numbers.

3. Play & count.

4. Play & sing (or say) the note names.

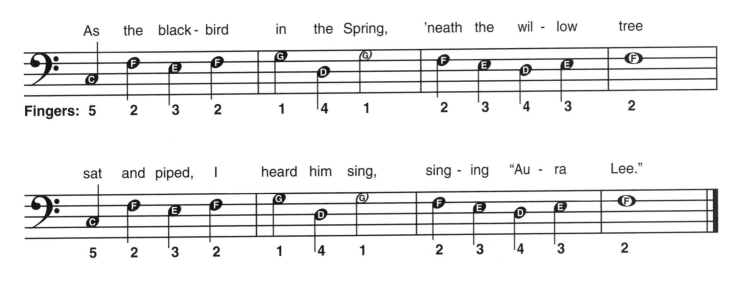

The Bass Clef Sign

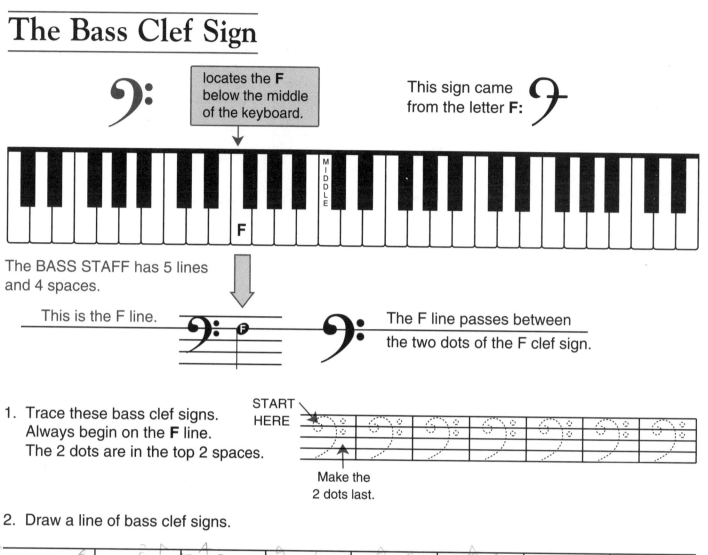

locates the **F** below the middle of the keyboard.

This sign came from the letter **F:**

The BASS STAFF has 5 lines and 4 spaces.

This is the F line.

The F line passes between the two dots of the F clef sign.

1. Trace these bass clef signs.
   Always begin on the **F** line.
   The 2 dots are in the top 2 spaces.

   START HERE

   Make the 2 dots last.

2. Draw a line of bass clef signs.

REVIEW

The notes of the LEFT HAND **C POSITION** are written on the **BASS STAFF.**

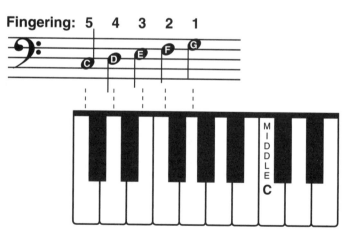

Fingering: 5 4 3 2 1

- The C, played by 5, is written on the second space of the staff.

- Each next higher note is written on the next higher line or space.

3. Write the names of the 5 notes in LH C position on the keyboard to the right.

4. Write the name of each note in the box below it.

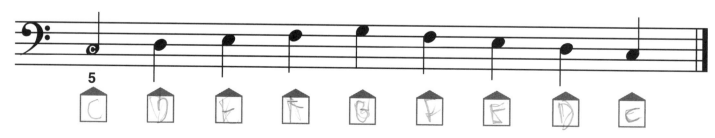

19

5. These notes are in SPACES. Write the name of each note in the box below it.

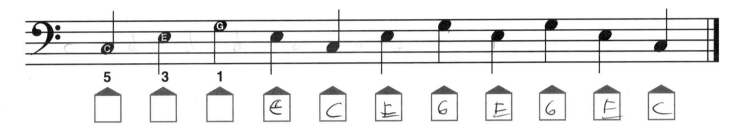

5   3   1

| | | | E | C | E | G | E | G | F | C |

6. These notes are on LINES. Write the name of each note in the box below.

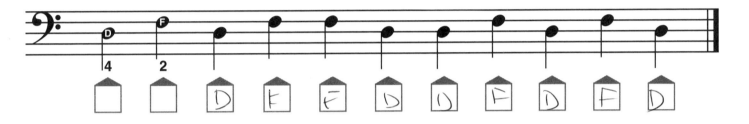

4   2

| | | D | F | F | D | D | F | D | F | D |

7. Here are notes on LINES & SPACES. Write the name of each note in the box.

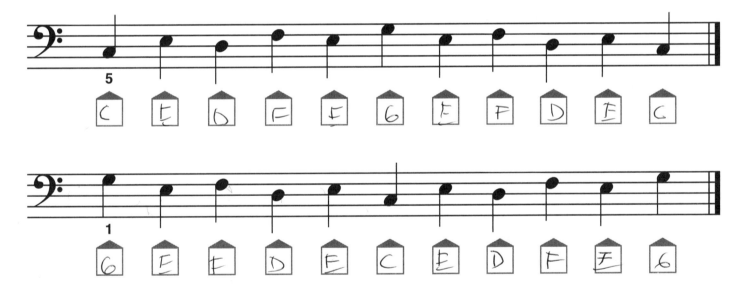

5

| C | E | D | F | F | G | E | F | D | E | C |

1

| G | E | F | D | E | C | E | D | F | F | G |

8. Each of these notes repeats on the SAME line or space.
Write the name of each note in the box below it.

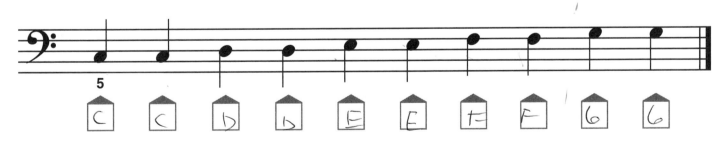

5

| C | C | D | D | E | E | F | F | G | G |

9. Below each note on this page, write the finger number used to play it in LH C POSITION.

10. Play all the notes on this page in LH C POSITION.

The Grand Staff

The BASS STAFF and TREBLE STAFF, when joined together with a BRACE, make up the **GRAND STAFF.**

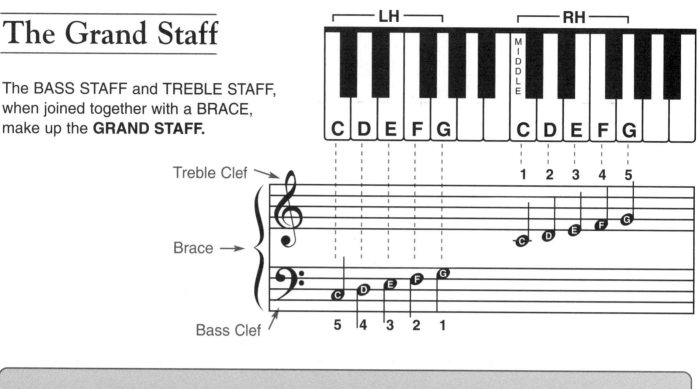

Treble Clef

Brace

Bass Clef

TIME SIGNATURE

Music has numbers at the beginning called the **TIME SIGNATURE.**

$\frac{4}{4}$ means **4** beats to each measure.

means a **QUARTER NOTE** gets one beat.

PLAYING ON THE GRAND STAFF

Only the starting finger number for each hand is given.

The following practice procedure is recommended for the rest of the pieces in this book:

1. Clap (or tap) & count.
2. Play & count.
3. Play & sing the words, if any.

This sign ▬ is a **WHOLE REST.**
LH is silent a whole measure!

RH silent a whole measure.

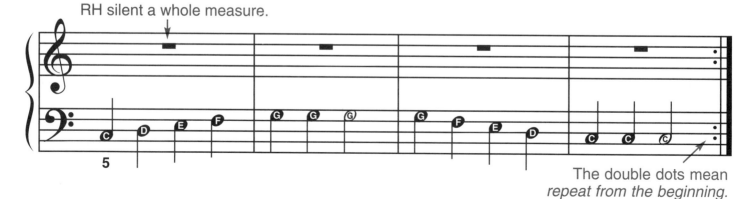

The double dots mean
repeat from the beginning.

Rock-Along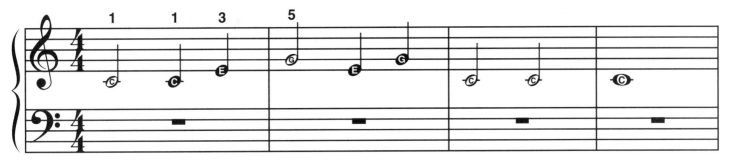

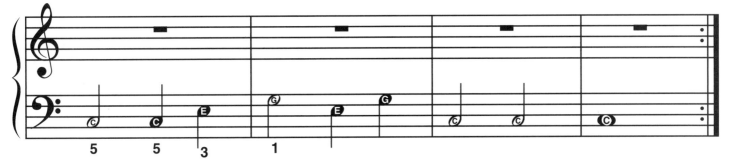

Mexican Hat Dance

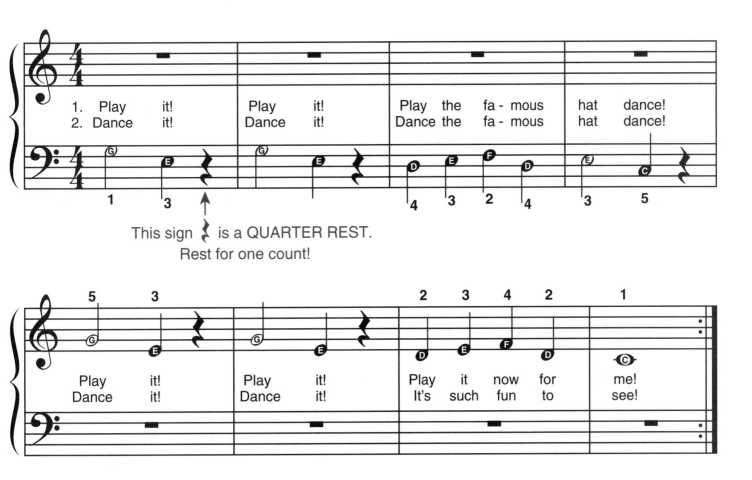

This sign 𝄽 is a QUARTER REST.
Rest for one count!

Writing in $\frac{4}{4}$ Time

Remember: Music has numbers at the beginning called the **TIME SIGNATURE.**

The **TOP NUMBER** tells the number of beats (counts) in each measure.

The **BOTTOM NUMBER** tells the kind of note that gets ONE beat (count).

$\frac{4}{4}$ = **4** beats to each measure.

= **QUARTER NOTE** gets ONE beat.

	NOTE	COUNT	Total number of counts
QUARTER	♩	"1"	1
HALF	𝅗𝅥	"1 - 2"	2
WHOLE	𝅝	"1 - 2 - 3 - 4"	4

1. In the box under each note, write the number of counts the note receives.

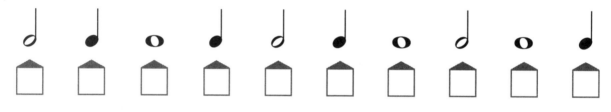

BAR LINES divide the music into MEASURES. Each measure in $\frac{4}{4}$ time has notes adding up to 4 counts.

2. Complete each measure by adding just one **G** to each, so the counts add up to 4:

3. Complete each measure by adding just one **C** to each, so the counts add up to 4:

4. Complete each measure by adding just one **F** to each, so the counts add up to 4:

LIGHTLY ROW 🔊9

1. Add BAR LINES like the first one shown, to divide the music into measures of 4 counts each.
2. Add a WHOLE REST in each measure to indicate silence for the LH or RH.
3. Write the name of each note in the box above it.
4. Play the piece.

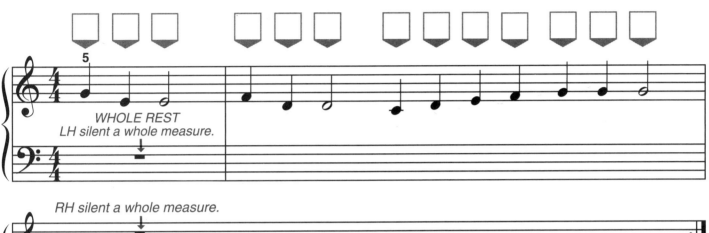

WHOLE REST
LH silent a whole measure.

RH silent a whole measure.

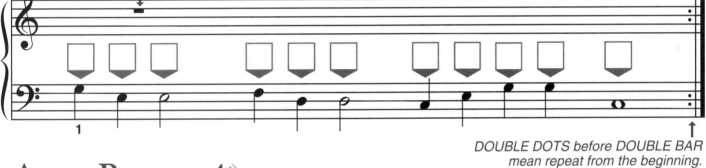

DOUBLE DOTS before DOUBLE BAR
mean repeat from the beginning.

AUNT RHODY 🔊10

1. Add BAR LINES dividing the music into measures of the correct length.
2. Add WHOLE RESTS as needed.
3. Write the name of each note in the box above it.
4. Add something before the last DOUBLE BAR to indicate that the piece should be REPEATED.
5. Play the piece.

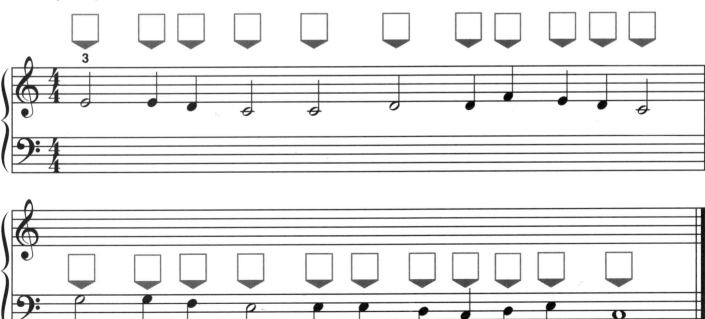

Melodic Intervals

Distances between tones are measured in **INTERVALS,** called 2nds, 3rds, 4ths, 5ths, etc.

Notes played *separately* make a *melody.*

We call the intervals between these notes **MELODIC INTERVALS.**

Play these MELODIC 2nds & 3rds. Listen to the sound of each interval.

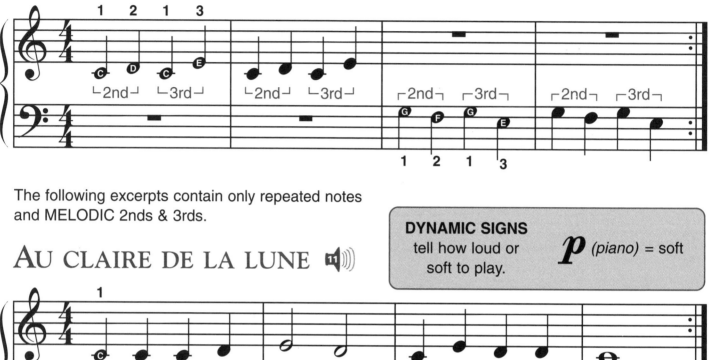

The following excerpts contain only repeated notes and MELODIC 2nds & 3rds.

AU CLAIRE DE LA LUNE

DYNAMIC SIGNS
tell how loud or soft to play.

p *(piano)* = soft

TISKET, A TASKET

mf *(mezzo forte)* = moderately loud

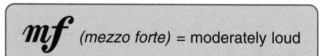

Measuring Melodic 2nds & 3rds

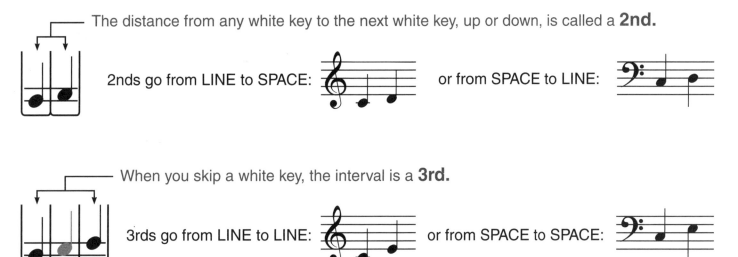

The distance from any white key to the next white key, up or down, is called a **2nd.**

2nds go from LINE to SPACE: or from SPACE to LINE:

When you skip a white key, the interval is a **3rd.**

3rds go from LINE to LINE: or from SPACE to SPACE:

Identify these intervals. If the interval moves UP, write UP in the top box. If it moves DOWN, write DOWN in the top box. Write the name of the interval in the lower box, as shown in the first two examples. If the note does not move up or down, write SAME NOTE.

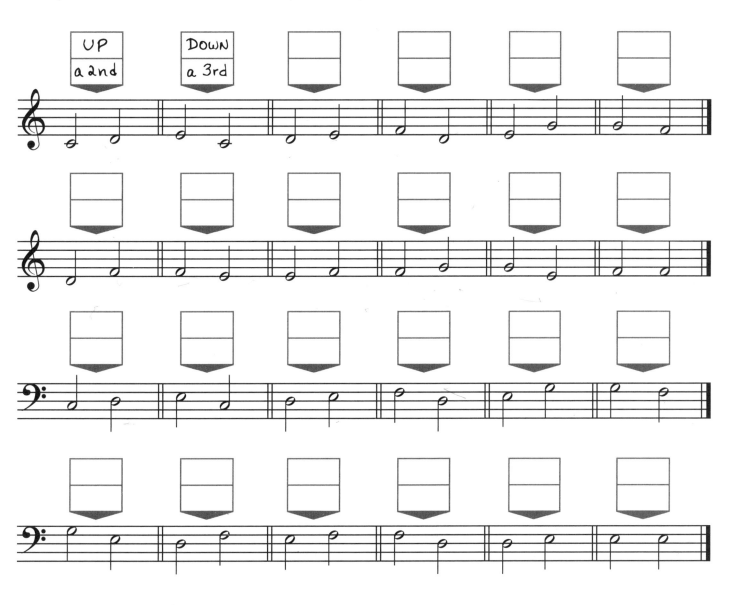

Harmonic Intervals

Notes played *together* make *harmony*.
We call the intervals between these notes **HARMONIC INTERVALS.**

Play these HARMONIC 2nds & 3rds. Listen to the sound of each interval.

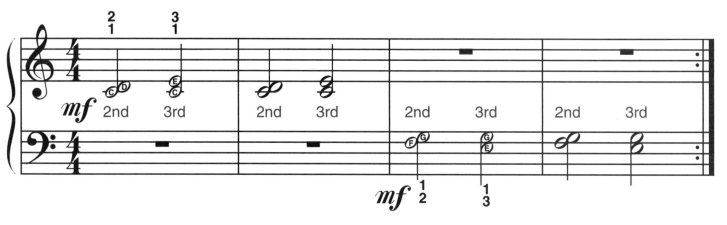

ROCKIN' INTERVALS 🔊

> f *(forte)* = loud

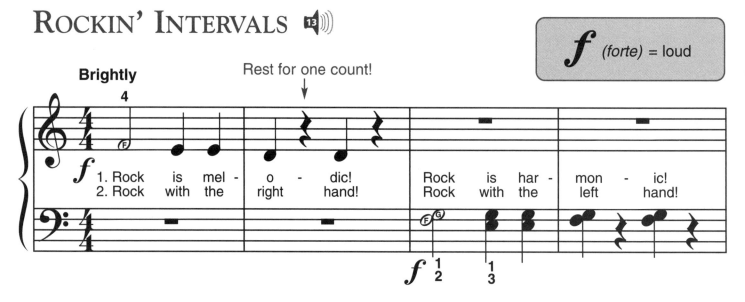

Brightly

Rest for one count!

1. Rock is mel - o - dic! Rock is har - mon - ic!
2. Rock with the right hand! Rock with the left hand!

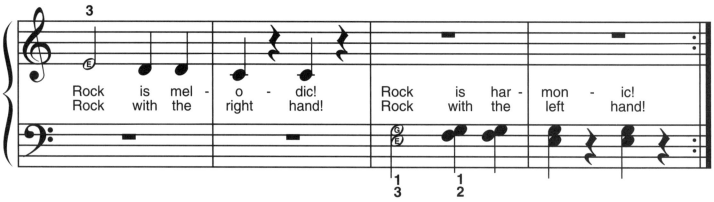

Rock is mel - o - dic! Rock is har - mon - ic!
Rock with the right hand! Rock with the left hand!

DUET PART: (Student plays 1 octave higher.)

RH

LH

Measuring Harmonic 2nds & 3rds

1. Play these HARMONIC 2nds & 3rds. Say the name of each interval as you play.

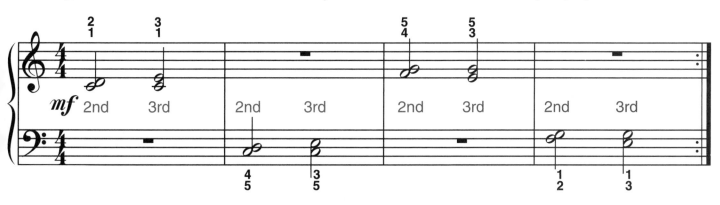

2. In the empty boxes, write the names of the notes that complete these HARMONIC INTERVALS:

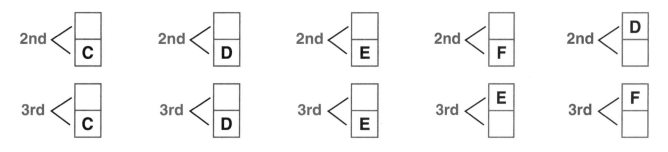

2nd $<$ ▢ / C   2nd $<$ ▢ / D   2nd $<$ ▢ / E   2nd $<$ ▢ / F   2nd $<$ D / ▢

3rd $<$ ▢ / C   3rd $<$ ▢ / D   3rd $<$ ▢ / E   3rd $<$ E / ▢   3rd $<$ F / ▢

HARMONICA ROCK 🔊14)))

3. Write the name of each harmonic interval in the box above it (2nd or 3rd).
4. Play, saying the name of each interval.

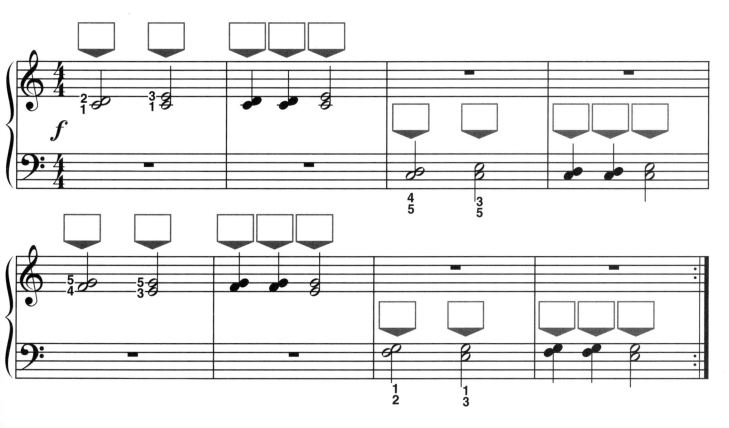

Melodic 4ths & 5ths

Play these MELODIC 4ths & 5ths.
Listen to the sound of each interval.

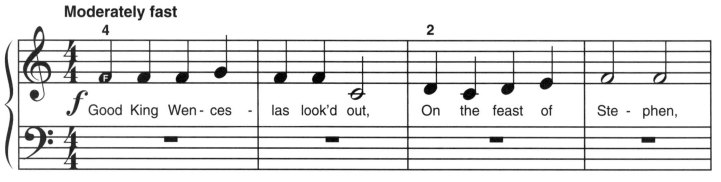

GOOD KING WENCESLAS 🔊 Find the 4ths before you play!

Moderately fast

Good King Wen - ces - las look'd out, On the feast of Ste - phen,

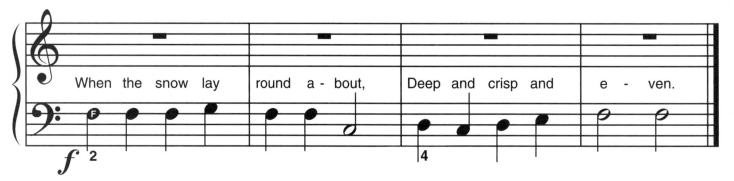

When the snow lay round a - bout, Deep and crisp and e - ven.

MY FIFTH 🔊 Find the 5ths before you play!

Seriously

This is my fifth, and may - be you've heard;

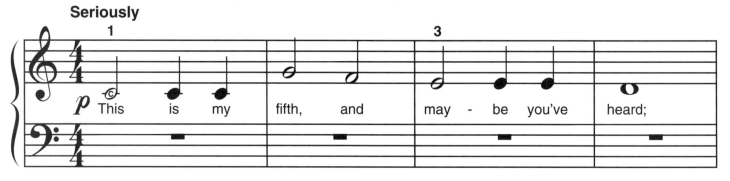

Beet - hov - en's fifth is on - ly a third!

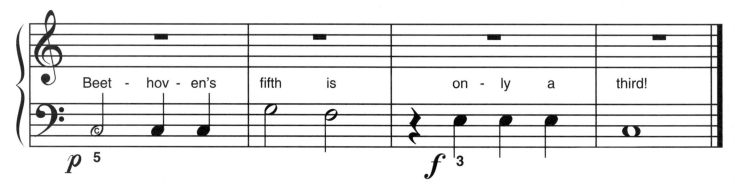

Measuring Melodic 4ths & 5ths

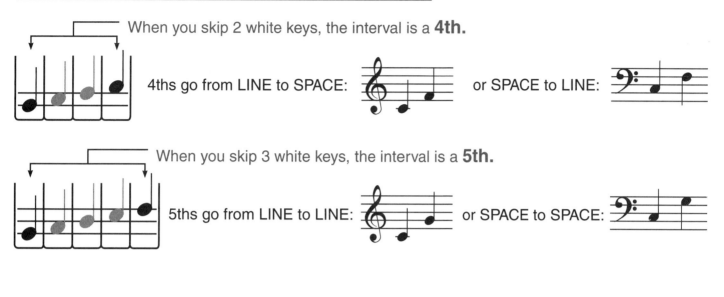

When you skip 2 white keys, the interval is a **4th.**

4ths go from LINE to SPACE: or SPACE to LINE:

When you skip 3 white keys, the interval is a **5th.**

5ths go from LINE to LINE: or SPACE to SPACE:

1. Write the names of the keys a 4th apart on this keyboard, beginning with the lowest F:

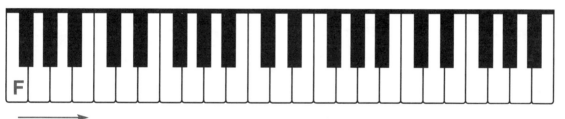

2. Write the names of the keys a 5th apart on this keyboard, beginning with the lowest F:

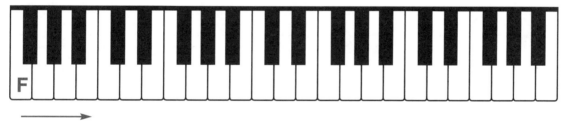

3. Identify these intervals. If the interval moves UP, write UP in the top box. If it moves DOWN, write DOWN in the top box. Write the name of the interval in the lower box. If the note does not move up or down, write SAME NOTE.

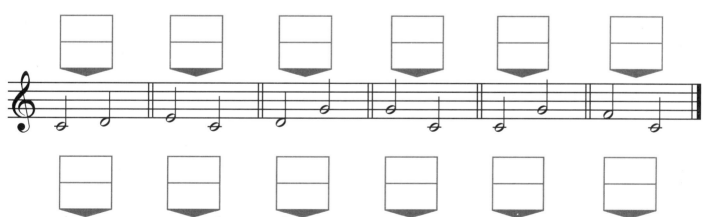

Harmonic 4ths & 5ths

Play these HARMONIC 4ths & 5ths.
Listen to the sound of each interval.

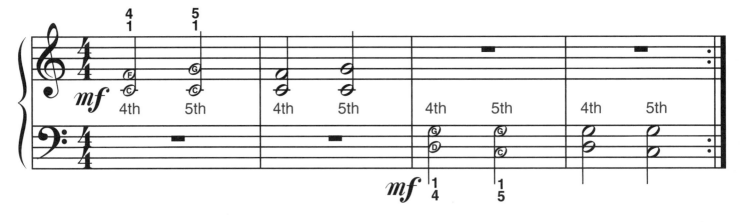

JINGLE BELLS

Before you play: 1. Find all the MELODIC 4ths & 5ths in the RH.
2. Find all the HARMONIC 4ths & 5ths in the LH.

Merrily

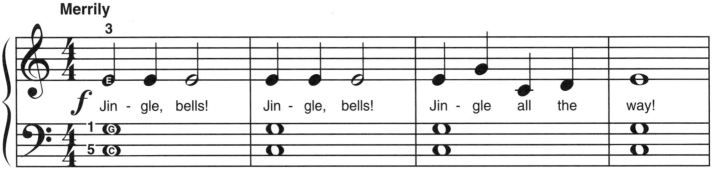

Jin - gle, bells! Jin - gle, bells! Jin - gle all the way!

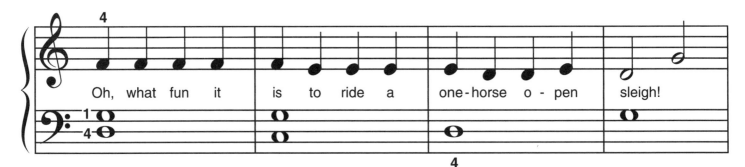

Oh, what fun it is to ride a one-horse o - pen sleigh!

Jin - gle, bells! Jin - gle, bells! Jin - gle all the way!

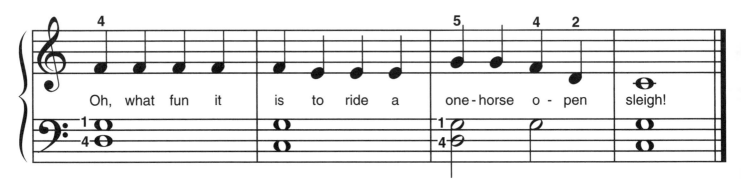

Oh, what fun it is to ride a one-horse o - pen sleigh!

Measuring Harmonic 4ths & 5ths

1. Play these HARMONIC 4ths & 5ths. Say the name of each interval as you play.

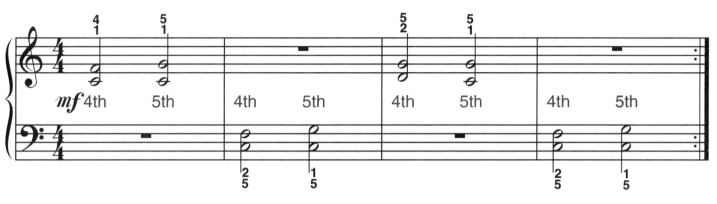

2. In the empty boxes, write the names of the notes that complete these HARMONIC INTERVALS:

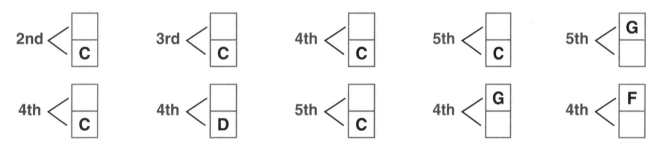

2nd   ◁   C   3rd   ◁   C   4th   ◁   C   5th   ◁   C   5th   ◁   G

4th   ◁   C   4th   ◁   D   5th   ◁   C   4th   ◁   G   4th   ◁   F

DUELING HARMONICS 🔊18

3. Write the name of each harmonic interval in the box above it.

4. Play, saying the name of each interval.

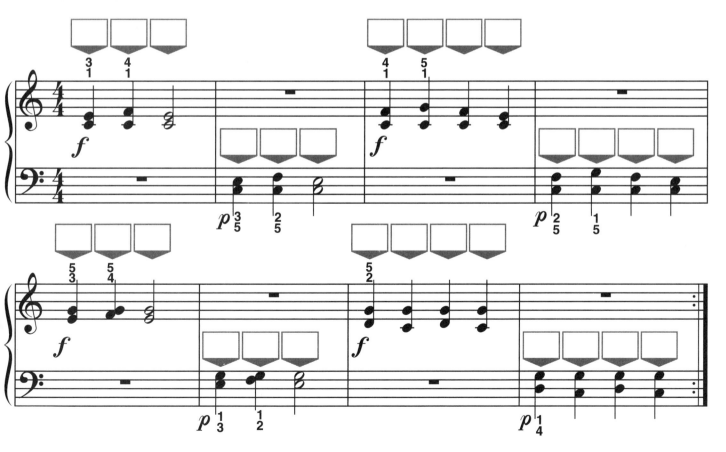

The C Major Chord

A chord is three or more notes played together.

The **C MAJOR CHORD** is made of three notes: **C E G.**

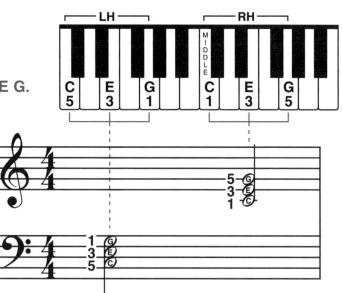

Be sure to play all three chord notes
exactly together, with fingers nicely curved.

C MAJOR CHORDS for LH

Play & count.

C MAJOR CHORDS for RH

Play & count.

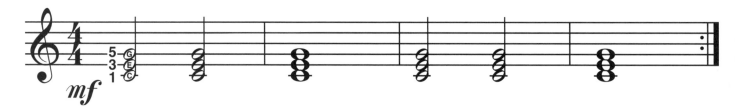

C MAJOR CHORDS for BOTH HANDS

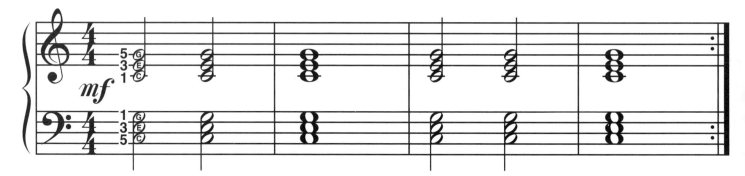

BROTHER JOHN

Read by patterns! For RH, think: "C, up a 2nd, up a 2nd, down a 3rd," etc. *Think* the pattern, then *play* it!

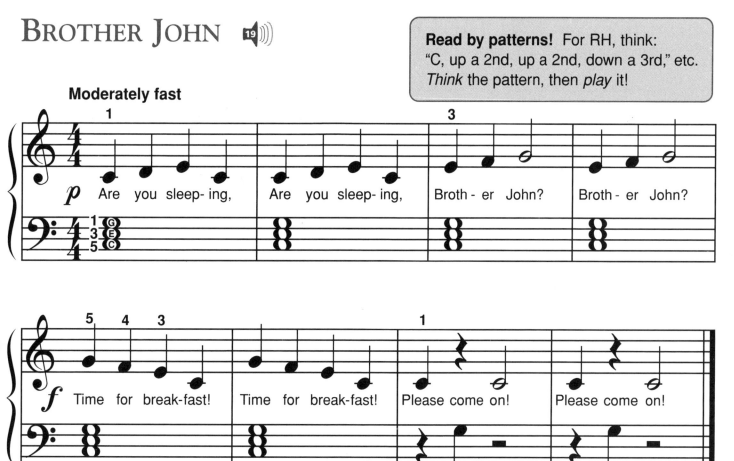

This sign ▬ is a HALF REST. Rest for two counts!

HERE'S A HAPPY SONG!

Read by patterns! For LH, think: "G, down a 2nd, down a 2nd," etc.

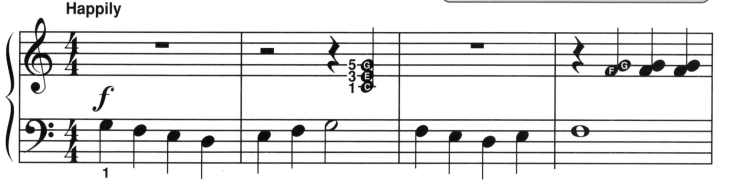

Introducing B for Left Hand

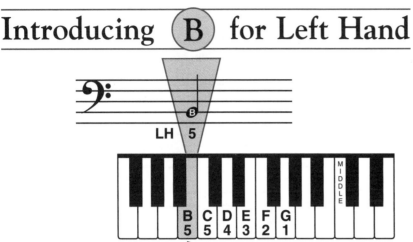

TO FIND B:

Place the LH in **C POSITION**.

Reach finger 5 one white key to the left!

Play slowly. Say the note names as you play.

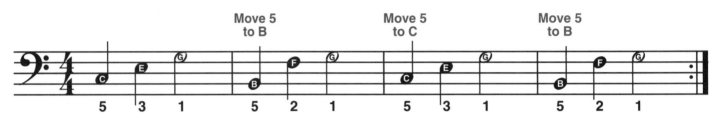

Two Important Chords

Two frequently used chords are **C MAJOR** & **G⁷**.

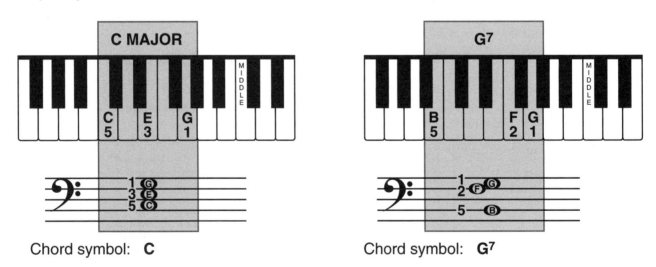

Chord symbol: **C**   Chord symbol: **G⁷**

Chord symbols are always used in popular music to identify chord names.

Practice changing from the C chord to the G⁷ chord and back again:

1. The 1st finger plays G in both chords.
2. The 2nd finger plays F in the G⁷ chord.
3. Only the 5th finger moves out of C POSITION (down to B) for G⁷.

TIED NOTES: When notes on the *same* line or space are joined with a curved line, we call them *tied notes.*

The key is held down for the
COMBINED VALUES OF BOTH NOTES!

Count: "1 - 2 - 3 - 4, 1 - 2 - 3 - 4."

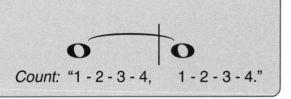

MERRILY WE ROLL ALONG 🔊

Play the RH & LH separately at first, then together. Practice the RH *mf* and the LH *p*.
The melody should always be clearly heard above the accompaniment.

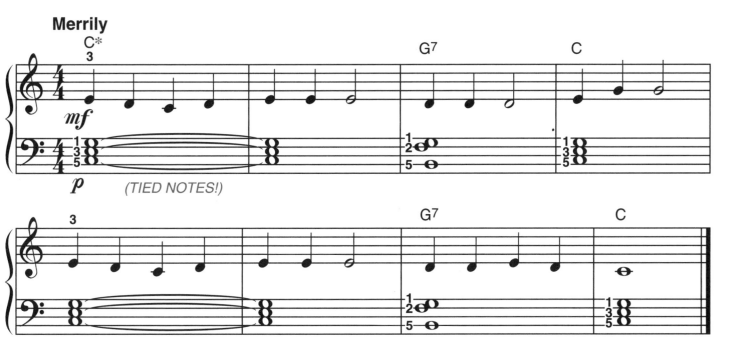

LARGO *(from "The New World")* 🔊

This melody is also known as "Going Home."

Dvořák

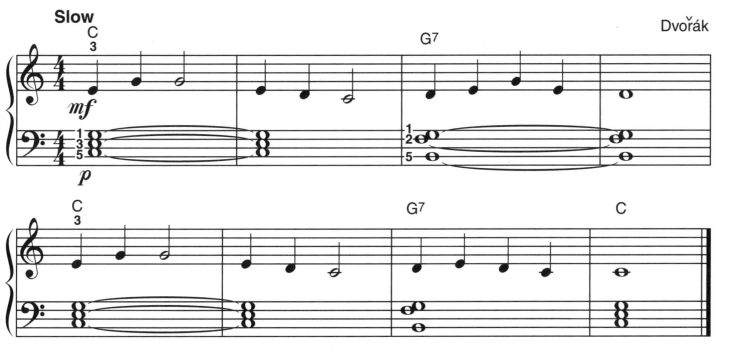

*In most popular sheet music, the chord symbols appear ABOVE the RH melody.
 The symbol appears ONLY WHEN THE CHORD CHANGES.

36

Introducing (B) for Right Hand

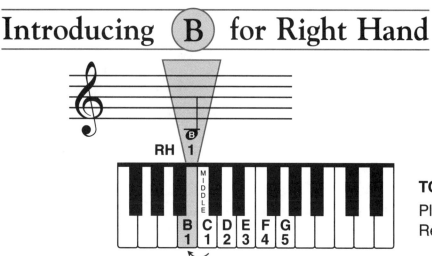

RH 1

TO FIND B:

Place the RH in **C POSITION.**

Reach finger 1 one white key to the left!

Play slowly. Say the note names as you play.

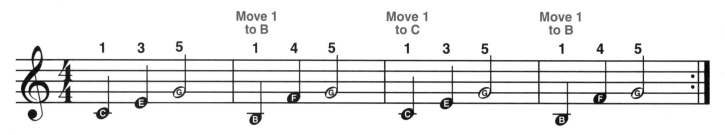

C & G⁷ Chords for Right Hand

It is very important to be able to play all chords with the RIGHT hand as well as the LEFT.
Chords are used in either or both hands in popular and classical music.

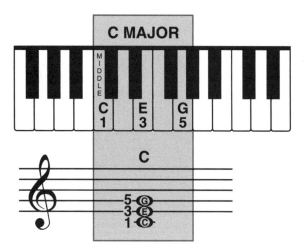

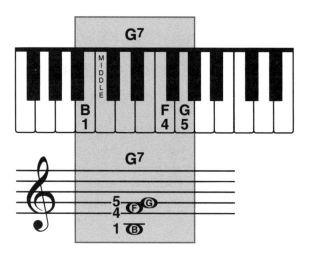

Practice changing from the C chord to the G⁷ chord and back again:

1. The 5th finger plays G in both chords.
2. The 4th finger plays F in the G⁷ chord.
3. Only the 1st finger moves out of C POSITION (down to B) for G⁷.

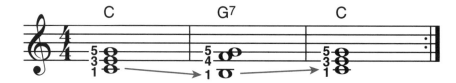

MARY ANN

Calypso tune

Moderately fast

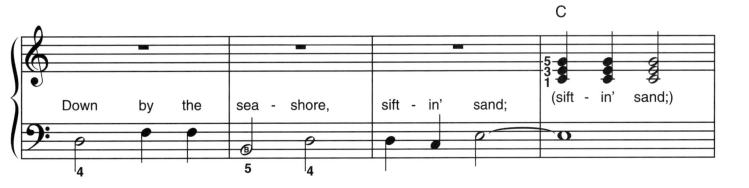

All day, all night, Ma - ry Ann, (Ma - ry Ann,)

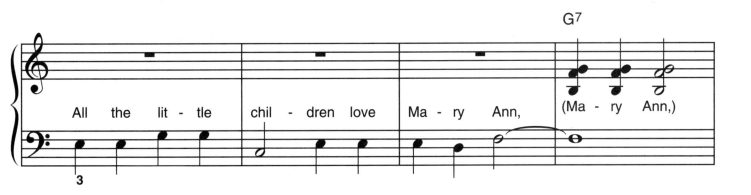

Down by the sea - shore, sift - in' sand; (sift - in' sand;)

All the lit - tle chil - dren love Ma - ry Ann, (Ma - ry Ann,)

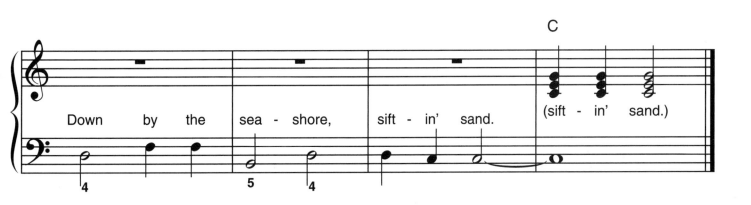

Down by the sea - shore, sift - in' sand. (sift - in' sand.)

The G⁷ Chord for Left Hand

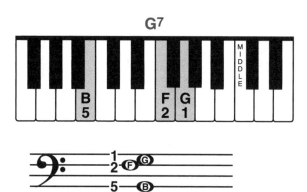

The construction of 7th chords will be more fully explained later. For now, the **G⁷ chord** will be made by playing **B F G** using LH 5 2 1.

It is easy to move from the C MAJOR CHORD to the G⁷ CHORD and back again, because both chords have the same G in common.

1. Practice changing from the **C** chord to **G⁷**.
   The COMMON TONE **G** is played by 1 in both chords.

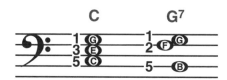

Chord Symbols

In popular music, chord symbols are used to identify chord names. The symbol for the C MAJOR chord is **C.** The symbol for the G SEVENTH chord is **G⁷.**

2. Write the chord symbols (C or G⁷) in the boxes below. Notice that a new symbol is used only when the chord changes.

3. Play and count.

4. Play and say the chord names.

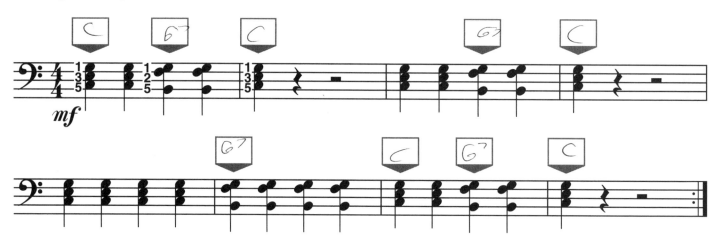

Remember: When notes on the same line or space are joined with a curved line, they are called TIED NOTES. Hold the key down for the COMBINED VALUES OF BOTH NOTES.

5. Write the chord symbols in the boxes.

6. Play and count. Say the chord names as you play.

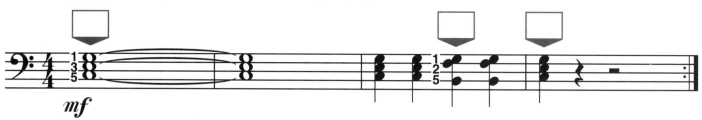

The G⁷ Chord for Right Hand

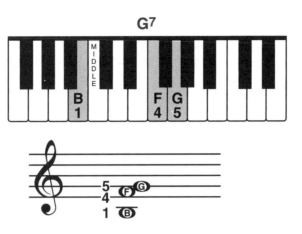

1. Practice changing from the **C** chord to **G⁷**.
   The COMMON TONE **G** is played by 5 in both chords.

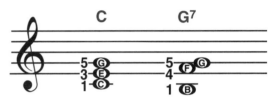

2. Write the chord symbols (C or G⁷) in the boxes below.

3. Play and count.

4. Play and say the chord names.

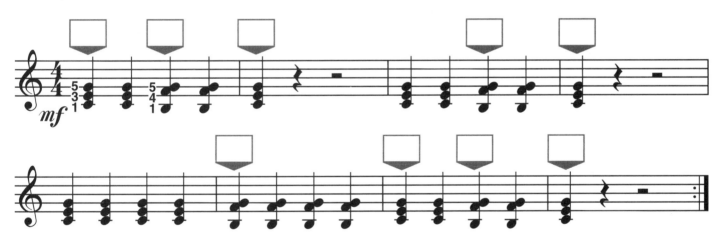

5. Write the correct chord symbols in the boxes below. Notice that when
   the GRAND STAFF (treble & bass staff together) is used, the chord
   symbols are written above the TREBLE STAFF.

6. Play and count. Say the chord names as you play.

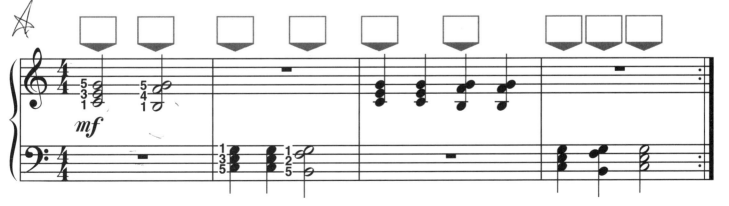

New Time Signature

Dotted Half Note

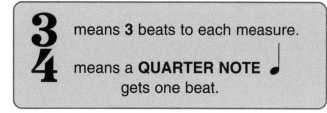

3 means **3** beats to each measure.

4 means a **QUARTER NOTE** ♩ gets one beat.

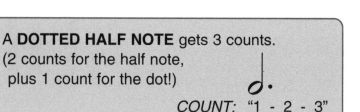

A **DOTTED HALF NOTE** gets 3 counts.
(2 counts for the half note,
 plus 1 count for the dot!) ♩.

COUNT: "1 - 2 - 3"

Clap (or tap) the following rhythm.
Clap **ONCE** for each note, counting aloud.

ROCKETS 24))

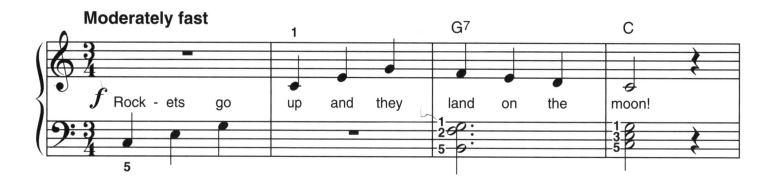

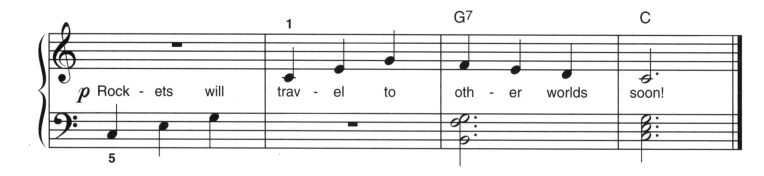

IMPORTANT! Play *ROCKETS* again, playing the second line one octave (8 notes) higher. The rests at the end of the first line give you time to move your hands to the new position!

Play *ROCKETS* one more time, now with the first line one octave higher than written, and the second line two octaves higher.

This is excellent training in moving freely over the keyboard!

Writing in 3/4 Time

1. In the box above each note, write the number of counts it receives.

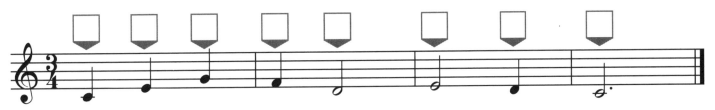

2. Check your answers. The notes in each measure of 3/4 time must add up to 3!

3. Under each line, write ONE NOTE equal in value to the sum of the TWO notes above it, as shown in the first example.

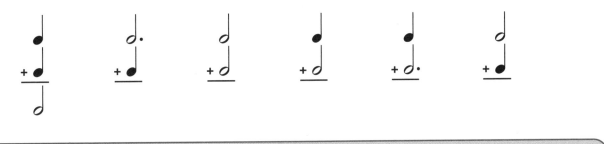

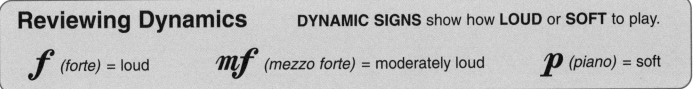

Reviewing Dynamics

DYNAMIC SIGNS show how **LOUD** or **SOFT** to play.

f (forte) = loud   *mf* (mezzo forte) = moderately loud   *p* (piano) = soft

4. Write the correct TIME SIGNATURE at the beginning of each of the following staffs.
5. Add CHORD SYMBOLS in the boxes above the treble staffs.
6. Play, carefully observing the dynamics.

Notice that a WHOLE REST is used to show silence for a whole measure of 3/4 or 4/4 time!

Moderately slow

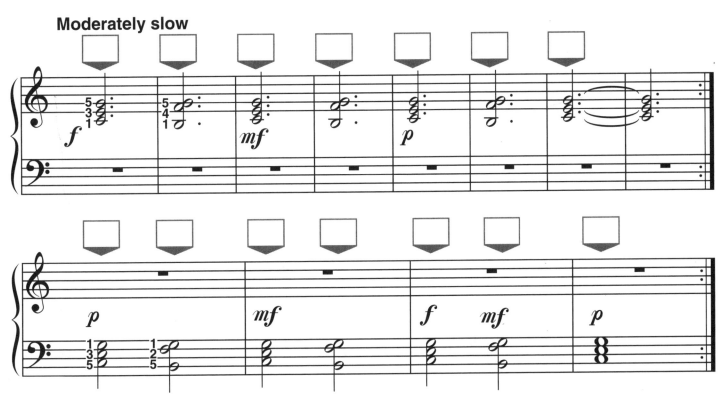

Slurs & Legato Playing

A **SLUR** is a curved line over or under notes on *different* lines or spaces.

SLURS mean play **LEGATO** (smoothly connected).

Slurs often divide the music into PHRASES.

A PHRASE is a musical thought or sentence.

What Can I Share?

Moderately slow

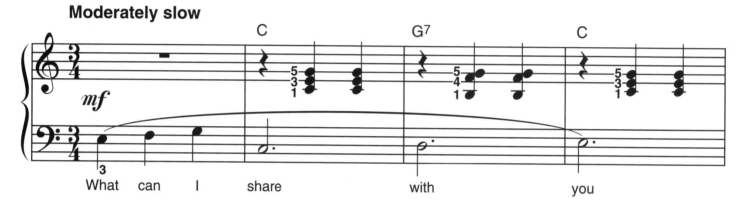

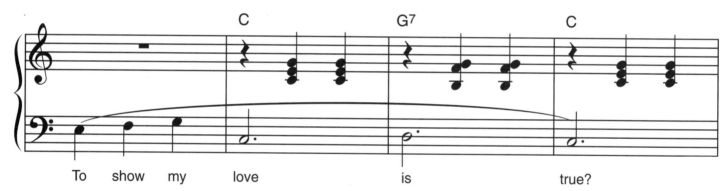

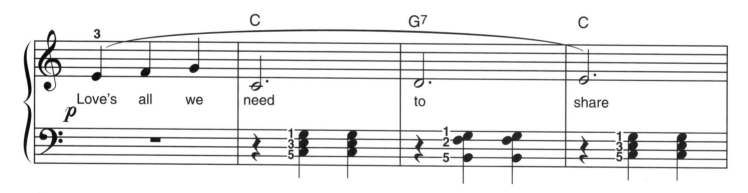

Day Is Done 🔊

1. Draw a slur over the notes that are played for the second sentence of the lyrics.
2. Play the RH, counting aloud.
3. Play the RH again, saying or singing the words. Connect the notes of each phrase as smoothly as you can.
4. Add CHORD SYMBOLS in the boxes above the treble staffs.
5. Play with hands together.

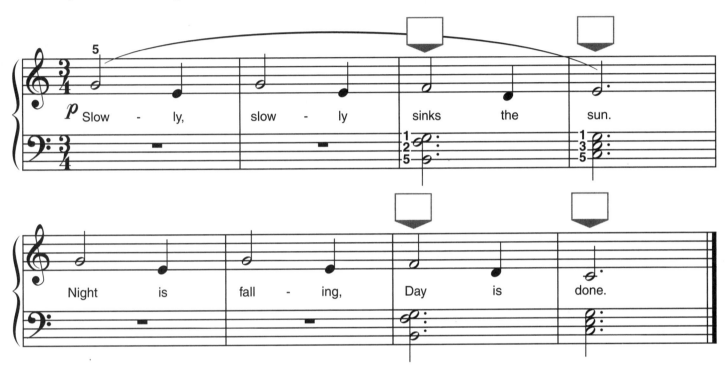

Slurs & Ties

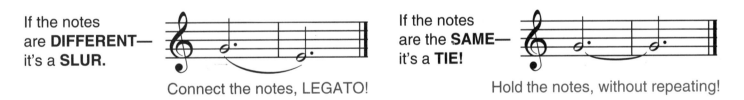

| If the notes are **DIFFERENT**— it's a **SLUR.** | If the notes are the **SAME**— it's a **TIE!** |
| Connect the notes, LEGATO! | Hold the notes, without repeating! |

6. Write **TIE** or **SLUR** in the box under each pair of notes, as shown in the first box:

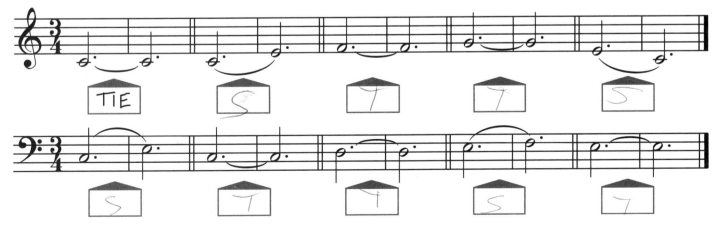

Introducing (A) for Left Hand

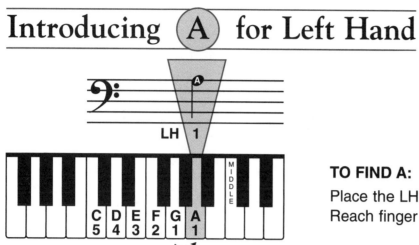

TO FIND A:

Place the LH in **C POSITION.**
Reach finger 1 one white key to the right!

Play slowly. Say the note names as you play.

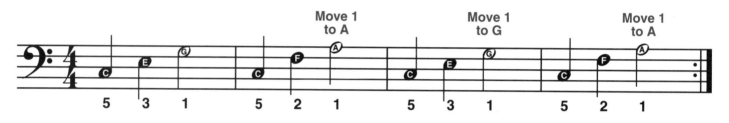

Introducing the F Major Chord

The C MAJOR chord is frequently followed by the F MAJOR chord, and vice-versa.

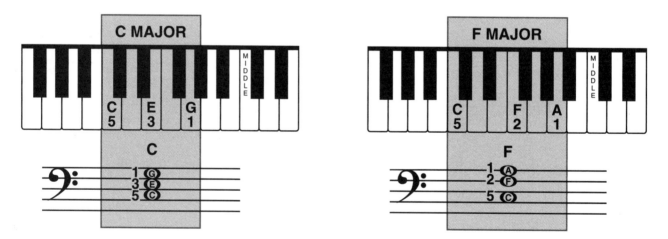

Practice changing from the C chord to the F chord and back again:

1. The 5th finger plays C in both chords.
2. The 2nd finger plays F in the F chord.
3. Only the 1st finger moves out of C POSITION (up to A) for the F chord.

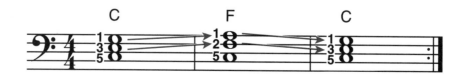

Warm-Up using C, G⁷ & F Chords

Practice SLOWLY at first, then gradually increase speed.

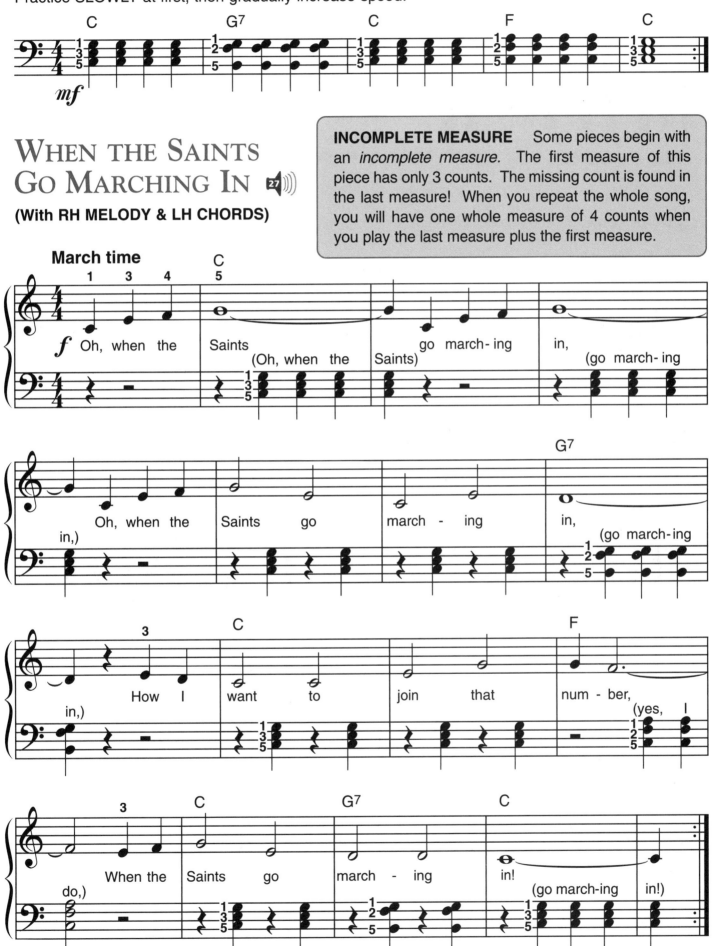

WHEN THE SAINTS GO MARCHING IN 🔊

(With RH MELODY & LH CHORDS)

INCOMPLETE MEASURE   Some pieces begin with an *incomplete measure.* The first measure of this piece has only 3 counts. The missing count is found in the last measure! When you repeat the whole song, you will have one whole measure of 4 counts when you play the last measure plus the first measure.

March time

Oh, when the Saints go march-ing in,
(Oh, when the Saints) (go march-ing in,)

Oh, when the Saints go march - ing in,
(go march-ing in,)

How I want to join that num - ber,
(yes, I do,)

When the Saints go march - ing in!
(go march-ing in!)

Introducing Ⓐ for Right Hand

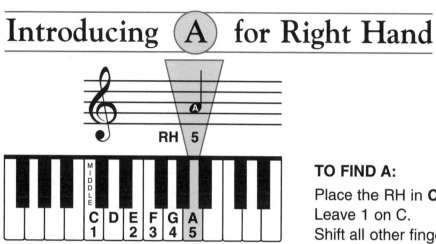

RH 5

TO FIND A:

Place the RH in **C POSITION.**
Leave 1 on C.
Shift all other fingers one white key to the right!

Play slowly. Say the note names as you play.

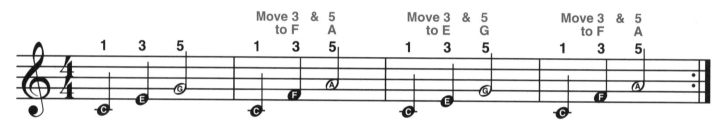

C & F Chords for Right Hand

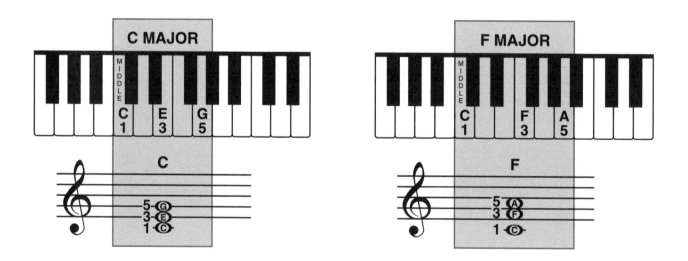

Practice changing from the C chord to the F chord and back again:

1. The 1st finger plays C in both chords.
2. The 3rd finger moves up to F and the 5th finger moves up to A for the F chord.

Warm-Up using C, G⁷ & F Chords

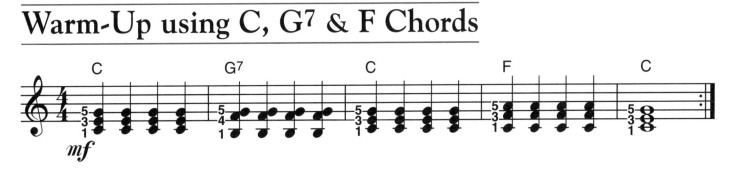

WHEN THE SAINTS GO MARCHING IN

(With LH MELODY & RH CHORDS)

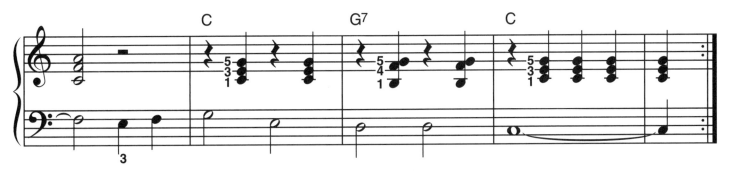

After you have learned both versions of *WHEN THE SAINTS GO MARCHING IN,* you will find it very effective to play page 45 followed immediately by page 47. Instead of playing the piece one way and repeating, you will be playing the melody first in the RH, then in the LH!

48

The F Major Chord for Left Hand

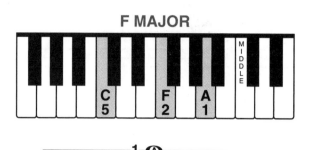

F MAJOR

The notes of the F MAJOR CHORD are **F A C.**

When moving from the C MAJOR CHORD to the F MAJOR CHORD, it is easier to play the F chord with the notes in this order: **C F A.** This allows the 5th finger to play C in both chords.

1. Practice changing from the C chord to the F chord. The COMMON TONE **C** is played by 5 in both chords.

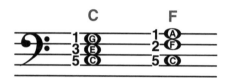

2. Write the chord symbols (C, F or G7) in the boxes.

3. Play and count.   4. Play and say the chord names.

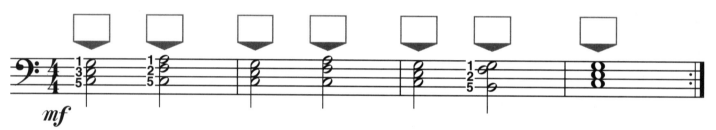

mf

I'M GONNA LAY MY BURDEN DOWN 🔊 29)))

This piece begins with an INCOMPLETE MEASURE of only 3 counts. The missing count is found in the LAST MEASURE!

5. Write the chord symbol in the box above each chord.

6. Play and count. Notice that the last incomplete measure plus the first imcomplete measure makes one COMPLETE measure when you make the repeat.

7. Play and say the chord names.   8. Play and say or sing the words.

Spiritual

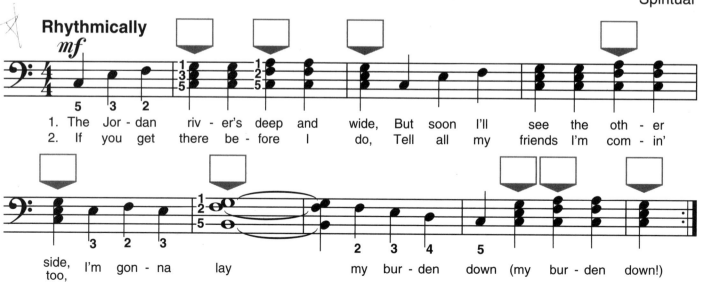

Rhythmically
mf

1. The Jor - dan riv - er's deep and wide, But soon I'll see the oth - er side,
2. If you get there be - fore I do, Tell all my friends I'm com - in' too,

I'm gon - na lay   my bur - den down (my bur - den down!)

The F Major Chord for Right Hand

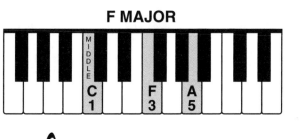

1. Practice changing from the C chord to the F chord.
   The COMMON TONE **C** is played by 1 in both chords.

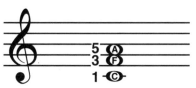

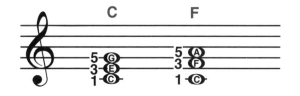

2. Write the chord symbols (C, F or G7) in the boxes.
3. Play and count.
4. Play and say the chord names.

WALTZING CHORDS

5. Write the chord symbols in the boxes.
6. Play and count.
7. Play, saying the chord name each time the chord changes.

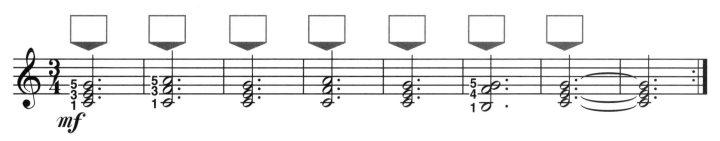

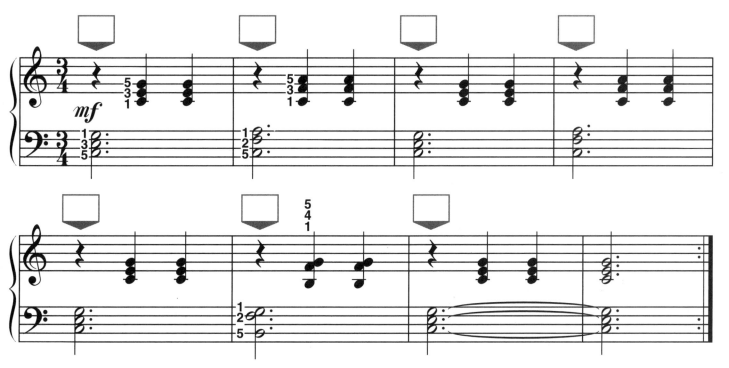

G Position

Until now you have played
only in the C POSITION.

Now you will move to the G POSITION:

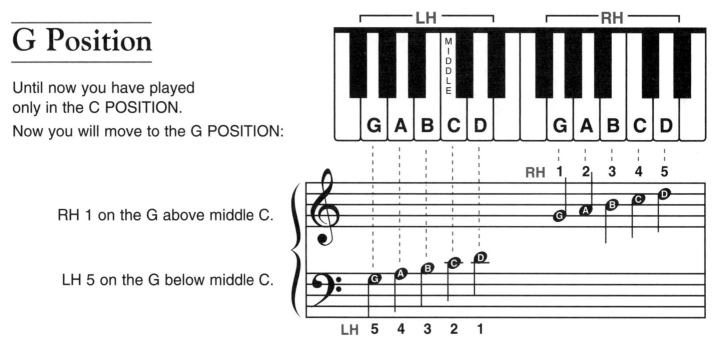

RH 1 on the G above middle C.

LH 5 on the G below middle C.

Play and say the note names. Be sure to do this SEVERAL TIMES!

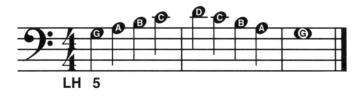 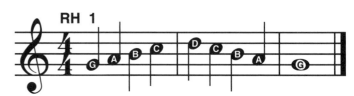

Intervals in G Position

1. MELODIC INTERVALS

Say the name of each interval as you play.

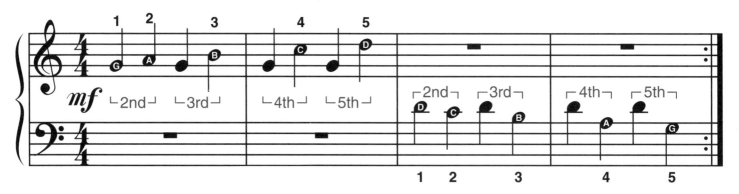

2. HARMONIC INTERVALS

Say the name of each interval as you play.

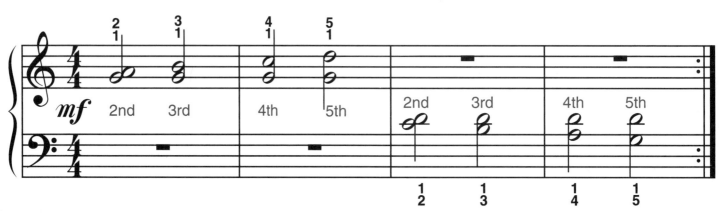

LOVE SOMEBODY! 🔊31

Before playing hands together, play LH alone, naming each harmonic interval!

A FRIEND LIKE YOU 🔊32

Before playing hands together, play LH alone, naming each harmonic interval!

Repeat with LH one octave (8 notes) lower.

Writing in G Position

RH 1 on the G above middle C.

LH 5 on the G below middle C.

THE BANDLEADER 🔊

1. Write the names of the notes in the boxes.

2. Play.

Moderately fast, like a march

f I'm the lead - er of the band. Out in front I proud - ly stand.

All I do is wave my hand; Out comes mu - sic loud and grand!

3. Write notes from the G POSITION that spell these words. The note values in each measure must add up to 4 counts. Turn note-stems DOWN when notes are ON or ABOVE the middle line of either staff. Turn note-stems UP when notes are BELOW the middle line.

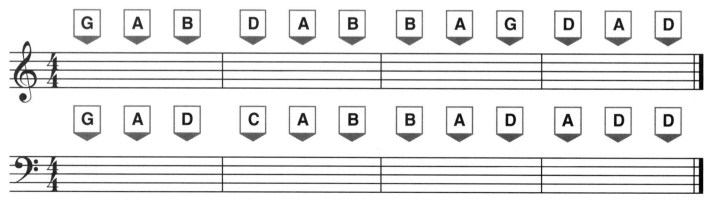

Melodic Intervals in G Position

1. Write the names of the notes in the boxes above the staffs.
2. Write the names of the intervals in the boxes below the staffs.

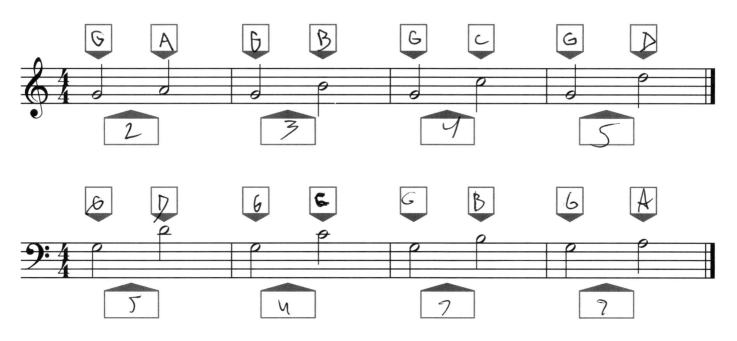

Harmonic Intervals in G Position

3. Write the names of the notes in the boxes above the staffs. Write the name of the lower note in the lower box and the name of the higher note in the higher box.
4. Write the names of the intervals in the boxes below the staffs.

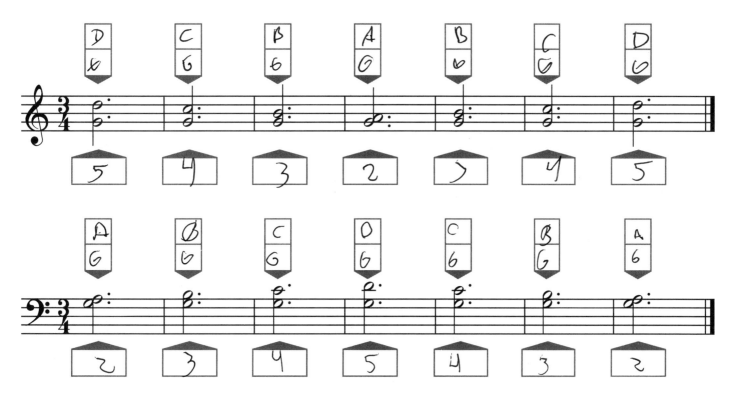

The Sharp Sign

 The **SHARP SIGN** before a note means play the next key to the RIGHT, whether black or white!

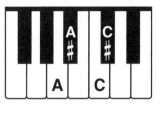

When a SHARP (♯) appears before a note, it applies to that note for the rest of the measure!

Circle the notes that are SHARP:

MONEY CAN'T BUY EV'RYTHING! 🔊 34

March time

Mon - ey can't buy ev - 'ry - thing! Mon - ey can't make you a king.

Mon - ey may not bring suc - cess; Mon - ey can't buy hap - pi - ness!

But of one thing I am sure: Mon - ey does - n't make you poor.

Mon - ey does - n't make you sad; Mon - ey can't be all that bad!

You are now ready to begin GREATEST HITS, Level 1.

Writing the Sharp Sign

1. Make some SHARP SIGNS:

   First, draw the two vertical lines.

   Then, add the heavy slanting lines.

   Draw 4 sharp signs here:

2. Write the names of the ♯ keys in the boxes below.

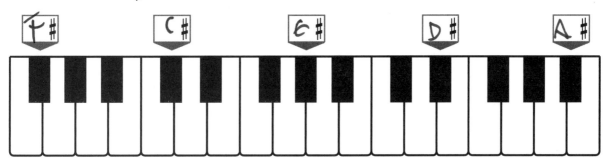

3. Change each of the notes below to a sharp note. Write the sharp sign BEFORE the note!

   When writing sharp signs, be sure the **CENTER** of the sign is on the line or space of the note to be sharped: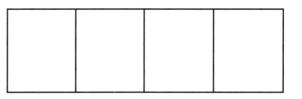

4. Write the name of each note in the box above it.

5. Play the notes, using RH 3 or LH 3.

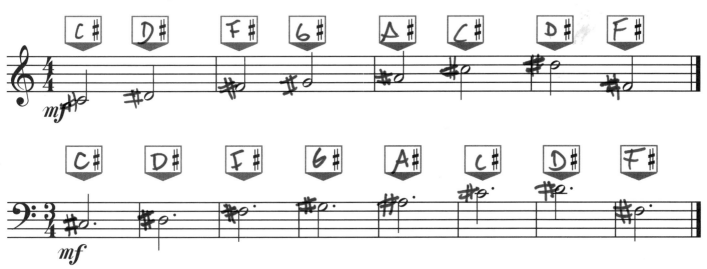

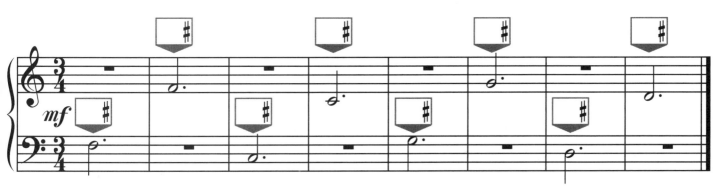

The Problem of Developing Equal Skills with All Fingers

By this time you will have realized that some fingers are more difficult to control than others.

The 5th finger is the smallest and weakest, and requires special exercise to develop strength equal to the others.

The 4th finger is the least independent finger, and the least agile. It is the only finger that is bound to its neighboring fingers by tendons that limit its movement.

The 3rd and 2nd fingers are the most agile fingers. They can move more easily through a larger arc. They are the strongest fingers.

The 1st finger (thumb) has its own problems. Its muscles are not designed to make it easy to strike a downward arc, but rather to pull the thumb inward, toward the palm. This makes it practical to turn the thumb under the fingers for playing scales, as you will see later, but in ordinary playing the thumb must strike on the side-tip, and is thus more awkward than the other fingers.

The following illustration shows the tendons of the left hand, as viewed from the back of the hand.

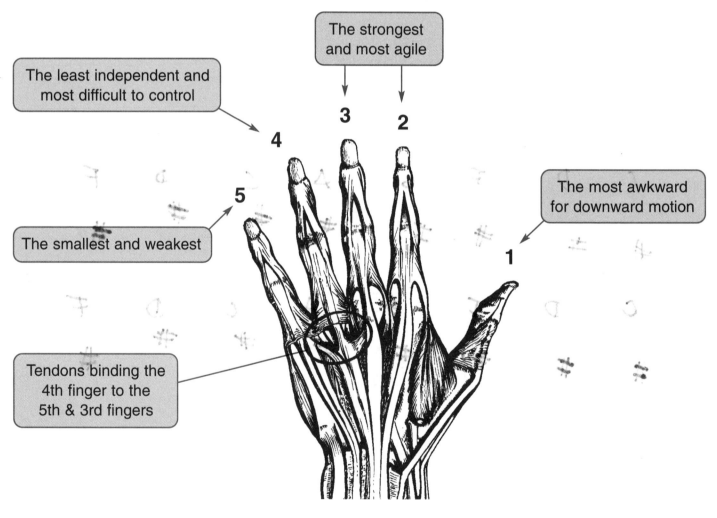

Illustration from Gray's Anatomy

A Leschetizky Solution

Theodor Leschetizky (1830–1915) was one of the most prestigious teachers of his time. Among his most famous pupils were Paderewski, Gabrilovich and Artur Schnabel. He was a genius at overcoming the technical problems of each of his pupils; one of his most effective exercises was specifically devised for developing skill and agility with all fingers, and overcoming the problems of playing well with the weakest and most awkward fingers.

IMPORTANT! Read Leschetizky's own instructions carefully before playing:

While FOUR fingers hold the whole notes down, ONE finger plays the quarter notes.
Repeat each measure many times.

1. In the first measure, press down the five keys together (G A B C D, all the keys in G POSITION), then raise the thumb JUST HIGH ENOUGH TO LET THE KEY RISE TO ITS LEVEL, keeping the thumb in touch with it. Now have the thumb press the key down again, hold it a moment, then rise again.

2. Continue in the same manner with the 2nd finger, raising it about one-third of an inch and striking the key repeatedly while the other fingers hold their keys.

3. Proceed similarly with the 3rd finger, keeping the others down.

4. Now continue with the 4th finger, but raise it AS HIGH AS POSSIBLE, so that this hampered finger may gain more independence.

5. Continue with the 5th finger, raising it also AS HIGH AS POSSIBLE, so that it may acquire more strength.

Keep fingers CURVED at all times.

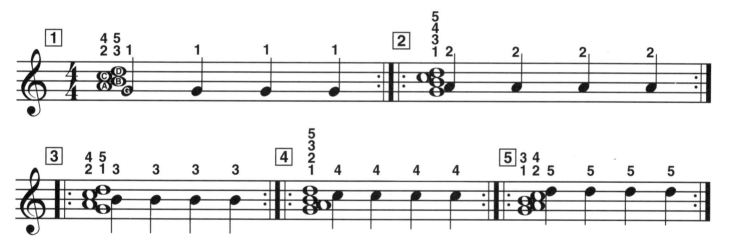

Follow the same procedure as outlined above when playing with the left hand.

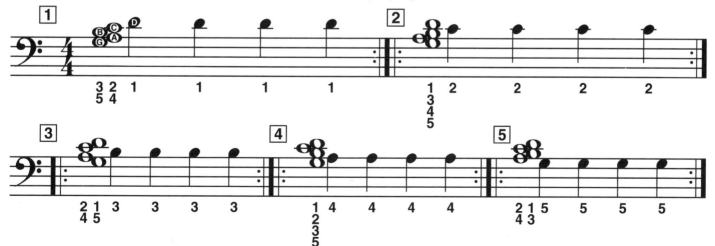

The G Major & D⁷ Chords for Left Hand

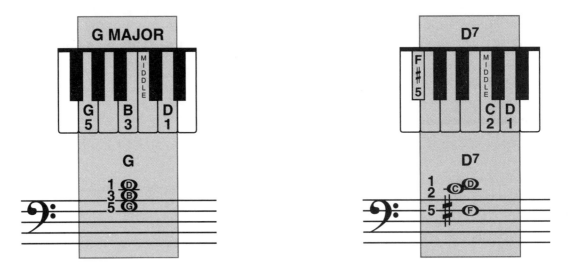

Practice changing from the G chord to the D⁷ chord and back again:

1. 1 plays D in both chords.
2. 2 plays C in the D⁷ chord.
3. Only 5 moves out of G POSITION (down to F♯) for D⁷.

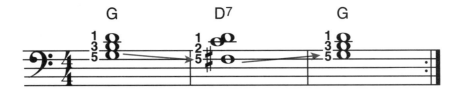

Play the following several times.

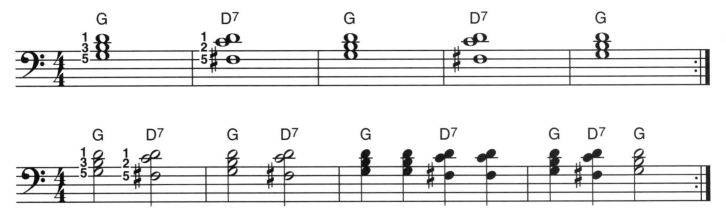

Preparation for *THE CUCKOO:*

THE CUCKOO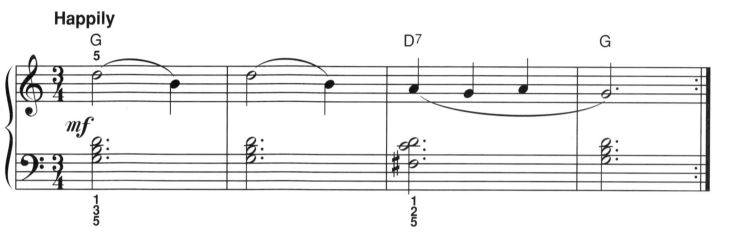

Happily

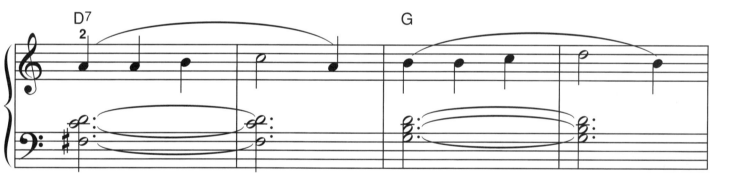

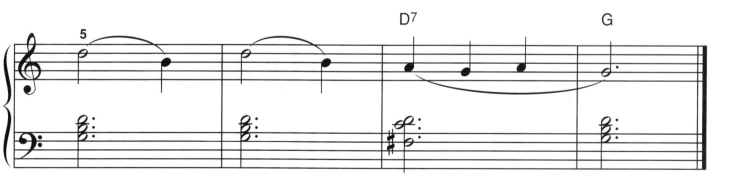

The G Major & D⁷ Chords for Right Hand

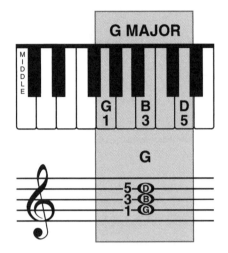
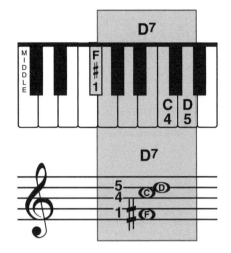

Practice changing from the G chord to the D⁷ chord and back again:

1. 5 plays D in both chords.
2. 4 plays C in the D⁷ chord.
3. Only 1 moves out of G POSITION (down to F♯) for D⁷.

Play several times:

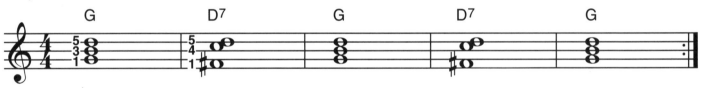

Block Chords & Broken Chords

When all three notes of a chord are played together, it is called a BLOCK chord.
When the three notes of a chord are played separately, it is called a BROKEN chord.
Play several times:

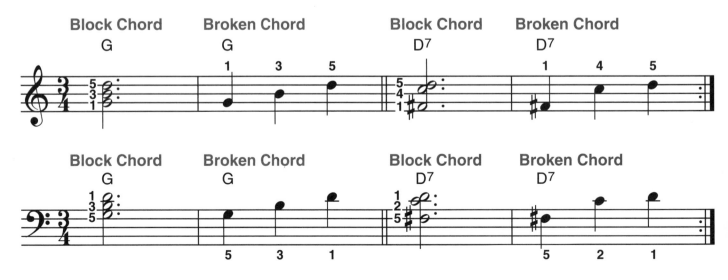

The Damper Pedal

- Use the RIGHT foot on the damper pedal.
- Always keep your heel on the floor.
- Use your ankle like a hinge.

The RIGHT pedal is called the **DAMPER** pedal.

When you hold the damper pedal down, any tone you sound will continue after you release the key.

This sign means: PEDAL DOWN   PEDAL UP

HOLD PEDAL

HARP SONG   Many pieces are made entirely of broken chords, as this one is!

Moderately slow

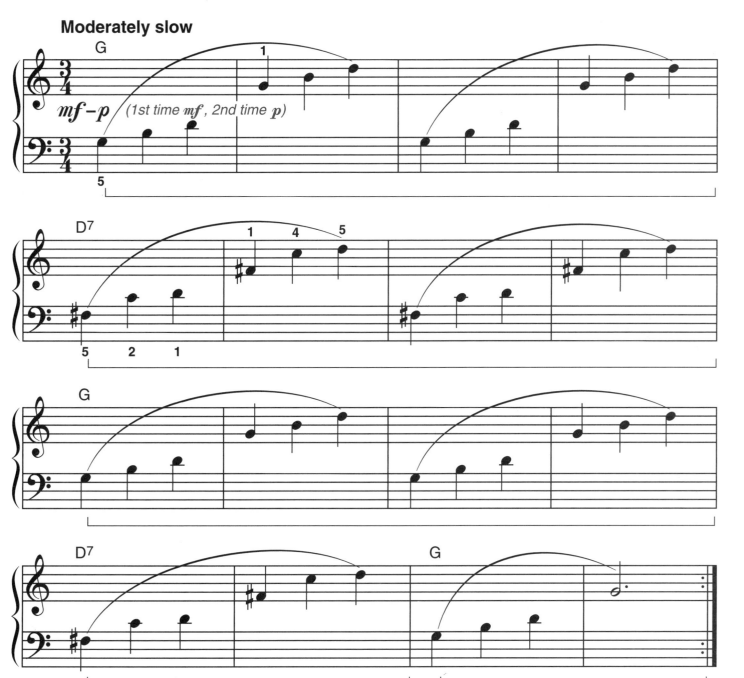

mf–p (1st time *mf*, 2nd time *p*)

Also play *HARP SONG* in the following ways:

1. Play the third and fourth measures of each line one octave higher than written.
2. Play the first and second measures of each line one octave lower than written.

Writing the G Major & D⁷ Chords for LH

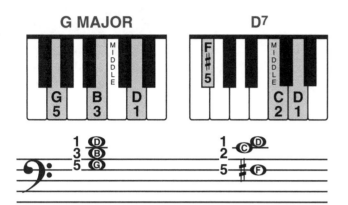

1. Practice changing from the G chord to the D⁷ chord. The COMMON TONE **D** is played by 1 in both chords.

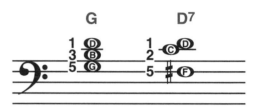

2. Write the chord symbols (G or D⁷) in the boxes below.
3. Play and count.
4. Play and say the chord names.

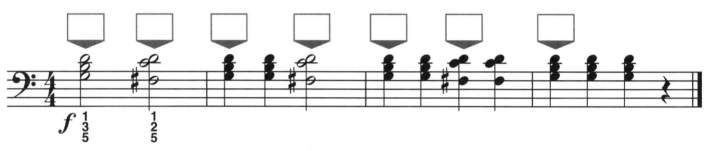

LIZA JANE 🔊

5. Write the chord symbols in the boxes below.
6. Play and count. 7. Play and sing or say the words.

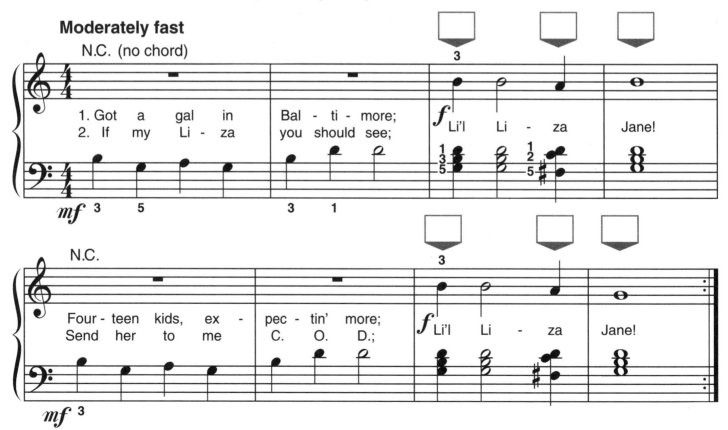

Moderately fast
N.C. (no chord)

1. Got a gal in Bal - ti - more; Li'l Li - za Jane!
2. If my Li - za you should see;

N.C.

Four - teen kids, ex - pec - tin' more; Li'l Li - za Jane!
Send her to me C. O. D.;

Writing the G Major & D⁷ Chords for RH

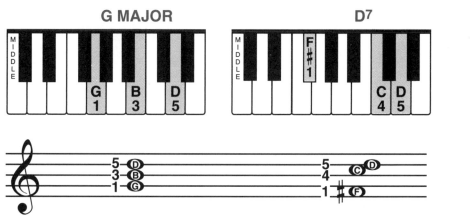

G MAJOR

D⁷

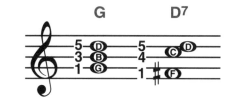

1. Practice changing from the G chord to the D⁷ chord. The COMMON TONE **D** is played by 5 in both chords.

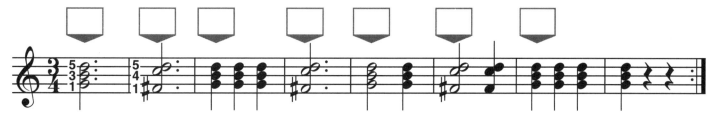

2. Write the chord symbols (G or D⁷) in the boxes below.

3. Play and count.   4. Play and say the chord names.

Block Chords & Broken Chords

BLOCK CHORDS: Notes are stacked VERTICALLY.
All notes are played TOGETHER.

G MAJOR & D⁷ BLOCK CHORDS:

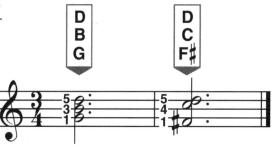

BROKEN CHORDS: Notes occur HORIZONTALLY, and are played SEPARATELY.

G MAJOR & D⁷ BROKEN CHORDS:

5. Write the names of the individual chord notes in the boxes above the staff.

6. Write BLOCK or BROKEN under each chord.

7. Play the chords with the LH.

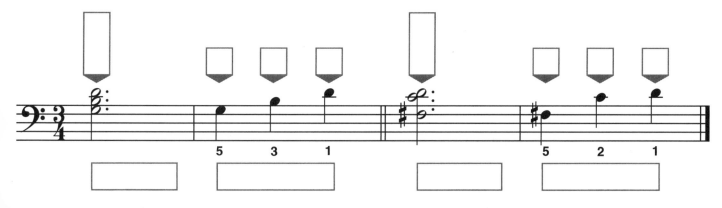

Introducing (E) for Left Hand

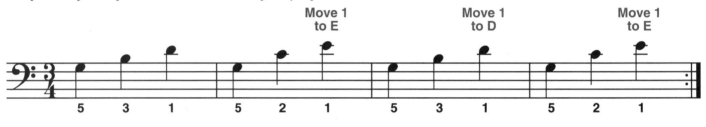

TO FIND E:

Place the LH in **G POSITION**.
Reach finger 1 one white key to the right!

Play slowly. Say the note names as you play.

A New Position of the C Major Chord

You have already played the C MAJOR CHORD with C as the lowest note: **C E G.**

When you play these same three notes in any order, you still have a C MAJOR CHORD.
When you are playing in G POSITION, it is most convenient to play G as the lowest note: **G C E.**

The following diagrams show how easy it is to move from the G MAJOR CHORD to the
C MAJOR CHORD, when G is the lowest note of both chords.

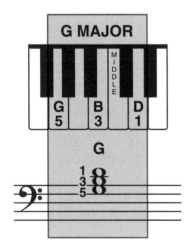

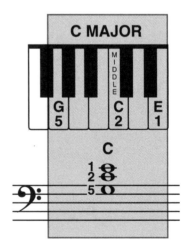

Practice changing from the G chord to the C chord and back again:

1. 5 plays G in both chords.
2. 2 plays C in the C chord.
3. Only 1 moves out of G POSITION (up to E) for the C chord.

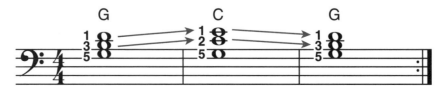

Warm-Up using G, D⁷ & C Chords

This warm-up introduces a new way of playing BROKEN CHORDS.

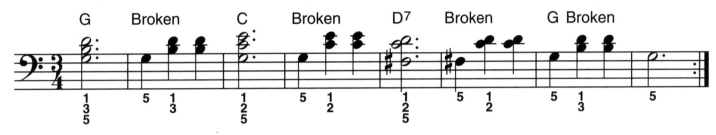

BEAUTIFUL BROWN EYES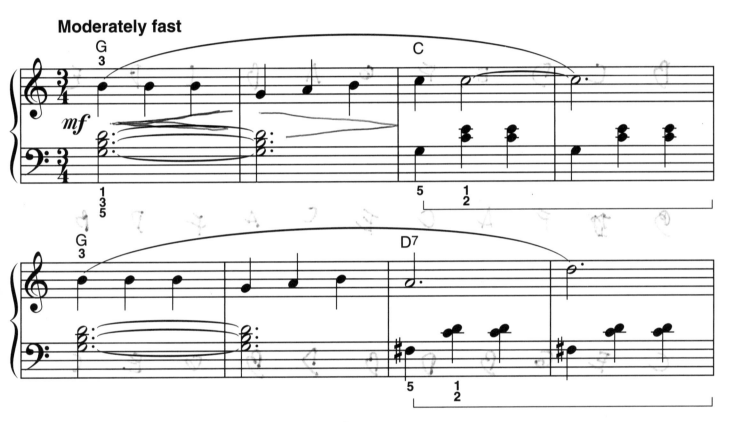

Moderately fast

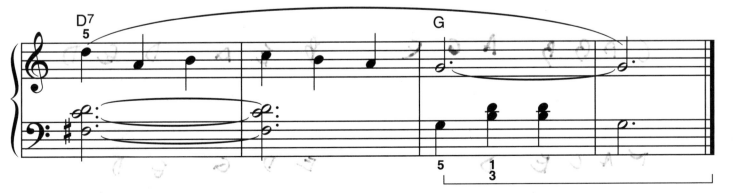

Writing Ⓔ for Left Hand

This reviews all LH notes studied so far!

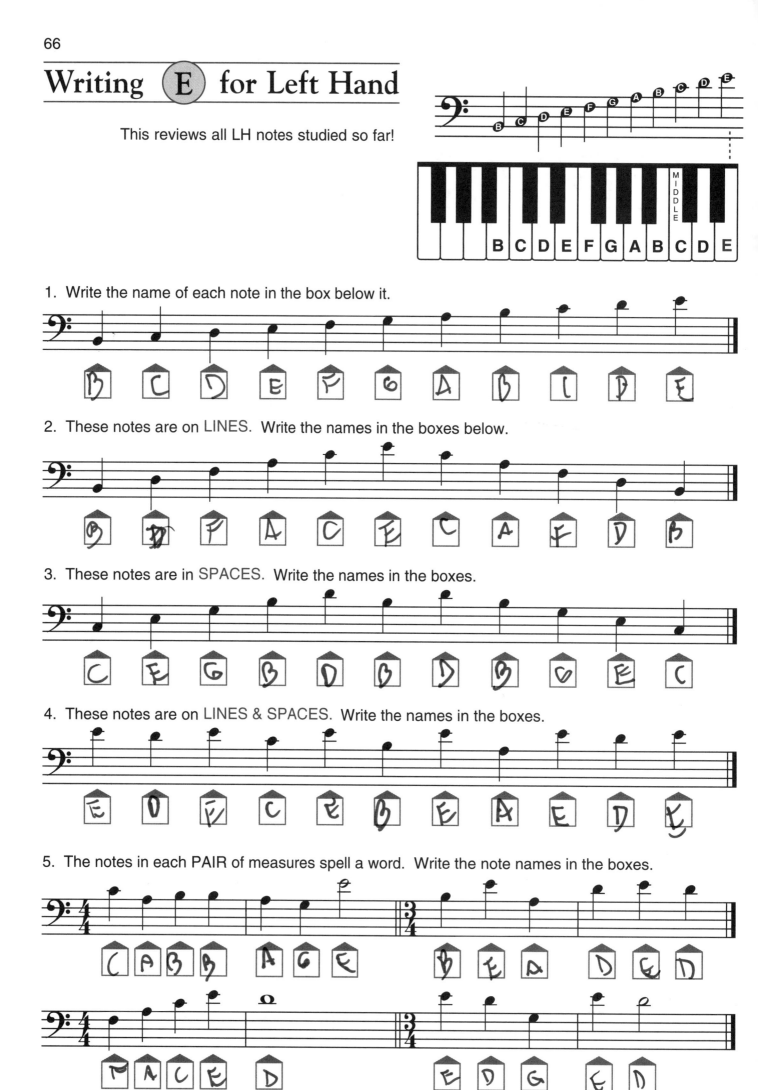

1. Write the name of each note in the box below it.

B C D E F G A B C D E

2. These notes are on LINES. Write the names in the boxes below.

B D F A C E C A F D B

3. These notes are in SPACES. Write the names in the boxes.

C E G B D B D B G E C

4. These notes are on LINES & SPACES. Write the names in the boxes.

E D F C E B E A E D E

5. The notes in each PAIR of measures spell a word. Write the note names in the boxes.

C A B B A G E   B E A   D E D

M A C E D   E D G E D

Writing the C Major Chord Position for LH

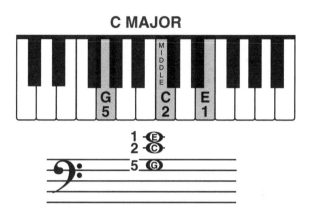

C MAJOR

REVIEW

You have learned that the C MAJOR CHORD contains the notes **C E G.**

When moving from the G MAJOR CHORD to the C MAJOR CHORD, it is easier to play the C chord with the notes in this order: **G C E.** This allows the 5th finger to play G in both chords.

1. Practice changing from the G chord to the C chord.
   The COMMON TONE **G** is played by 5 in both chords.

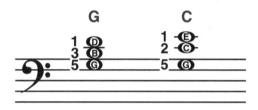

2. Write the chord symbols (G, C or D7) in the boxes below.

3. Play and count.   4. Play and say the chord names.

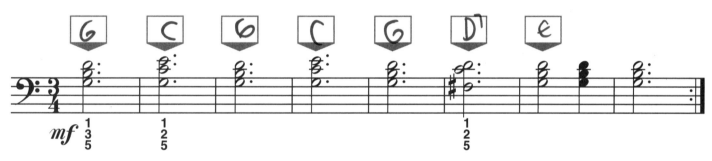

BROKEN CHORDS may be played several ways. Each note may be played separately, or one note may be played, followed by the remaining two notes.

5. Write the chord symbols in the boxes below. You will have to look at all the notes in each measure to determine the chord name.

6. Play and say the chord names.

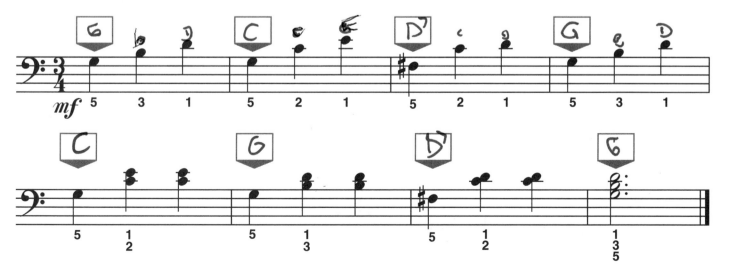

Introducing (E) for Right Hand

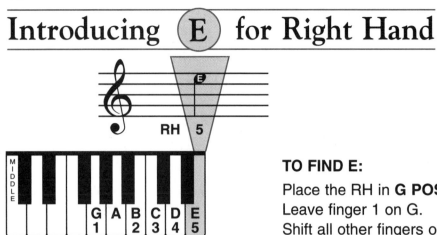

TO FIND E:

Place the RH in **G POSITION.**
Leave finger 1 on G.
Shift all other fingers one white key to the right.

Play slowly. Say the note names as you play.

New C Major Chord Position for Right Hand

Notice that *two* fingers must move to the right when changing from the G MAJOR CHORD to the C MAJOR CHORD.

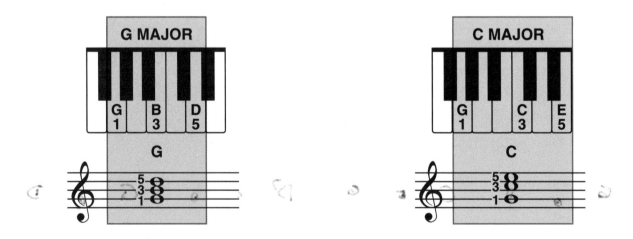

Practice changing from the G chord to the C chord and back again:

1. 1 plays G in both chords.
2. 3 moves up to C and 5 moves up to E for the C chord.

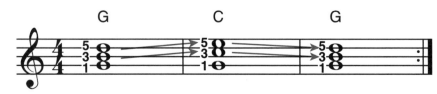

Warm-Up using G, D⁷ & C Chords

Play SLOWLY at first, then gradually increase speed.

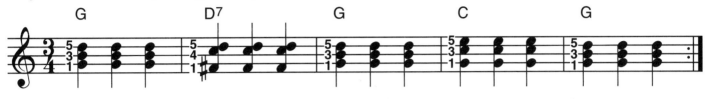

ALPINE MELODY 🔊39

The LH melody of this piece consists entirely of BROKEN CHORDS,
which are the same as the BLOCK CHORDS played by the RH in each measure!

Moderately slow

*Play both hands 8va
(one octave higher)
the 2nd time!*

Writing (E) for Right Hand

This reviews all RH notes studied so far!

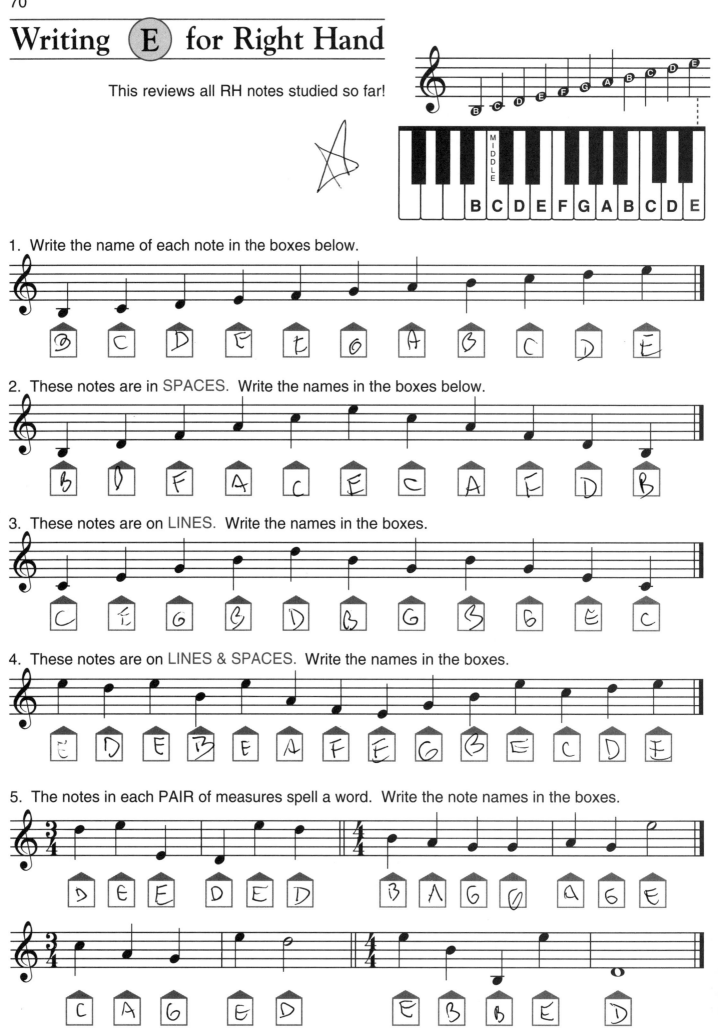

1. Write the name of each note in the boxes below.

B C D E E G A B C D E

2. These notes are in SPACES. Write the names in the boxes below.

B D F A C E C A E D B

3. These notes are on LINES. Write the names in the boxes.

C E G B D B G B B E C

4. These notes are on LINES & SPACES. Write the names in the boxes.

E D E B E A F E G B E C D E

5. The notes in each PAIR of measures spell a word. Write the note names in the boxes.

D E E D E D   B A G G A G E

C A G E D   E B B E D

Writing the C Major Chord Position for RH

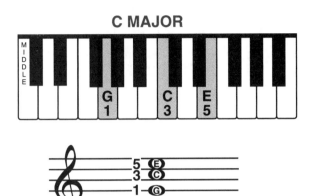

1. Practice changing from the G chord to the C chord. The COMMON TONE **G** is played by 1 in both chords.

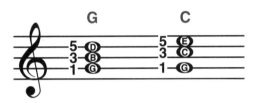

In this piece, both hands always play the same chords at the same time.
In the RH, the chords are BROKEN. The LH plays BLOCK chords.

2. Write the chord symbols in the boxes.

3. Play. Carefully observe all ties and pedal indications.

Moderately slow

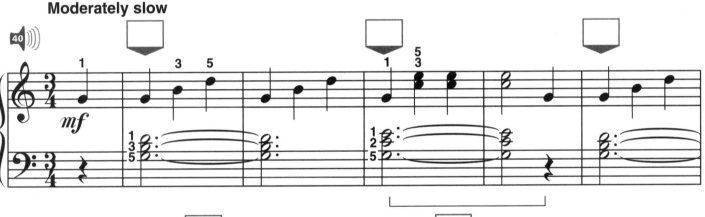

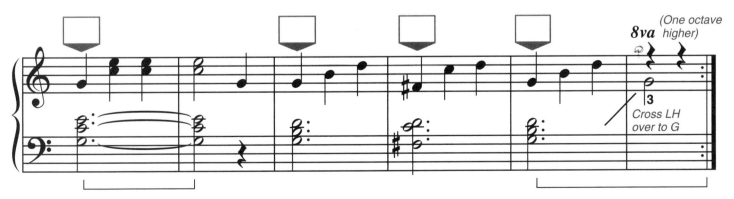

Middle C Position

The MIDDLE C POSITION uses notes you already know!

- RH is in C POSITION.
- LH moves one note down from G POSITION.
- Both thumbs are now on Middle C.

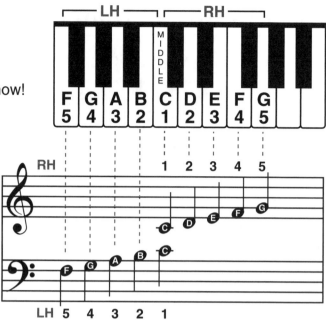

Play and say the note names. Do this several times!

THUMBS ON C! 🔊

Moderately slow

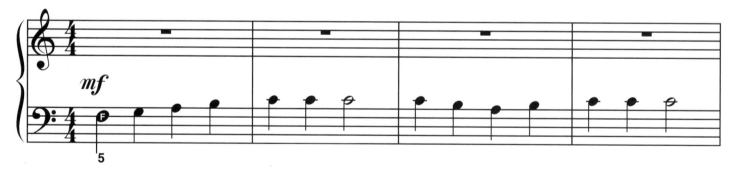

WALTZ TIME 🔊42

CONTINUE TO READ BY PATTERNS! For LH, think:
"C, same, down a 2nd, down a 2nd, up a 2nd," etc.

Moderate waltz tempo (tempo = speed)

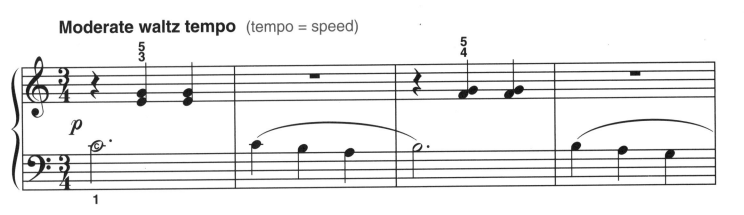

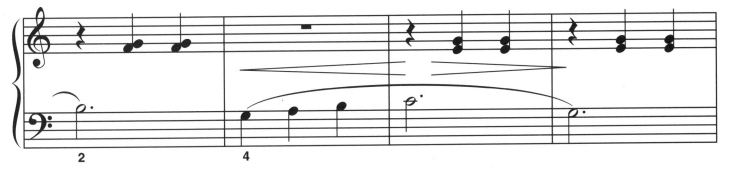

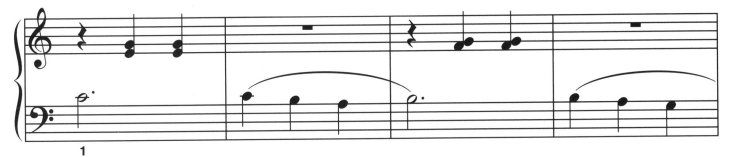

*Repeat with both hands 8va
(one octave higher).*

> This sign is called a **FERMATA.**
>
> Hold the note under the fermata *longer* than its value.

GOOD MORNING TO YOU! 🔊

MIDDLE C POSITION

Happily

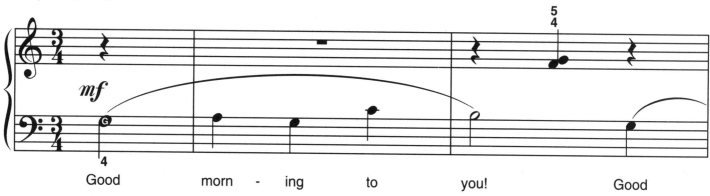

Good morn - ing to you! Good

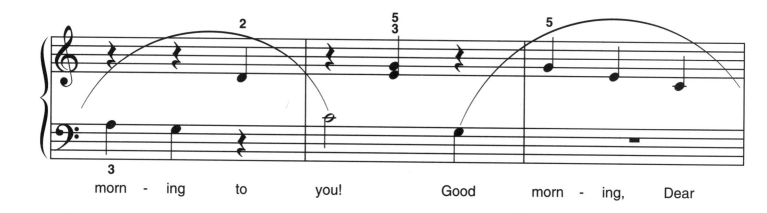

morn - ing to you! Good morn - ing, Dear

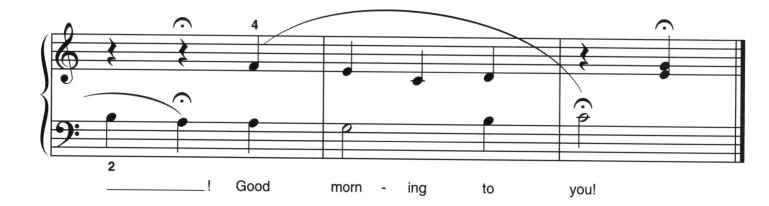

_____ ! Good morn - ing to you!

Eighth Notes

Two eighth notes are played in the time of **one quarter note.**

When a piece contains eighth notes, count:

"**1 - &**" or "**quar - ter**"   for each quarter note;
"**1 - &**" or "**two eighths**" for each pair of eighth notes.

Clap (or tap) these notes, counting aloud:

HAPPY BIRTHDAY TO YOU! 44

HAPPY BIRTHDAY is exactly the same as *GOOD MORNING TO YOU,* except for the eighth notes!

Happily

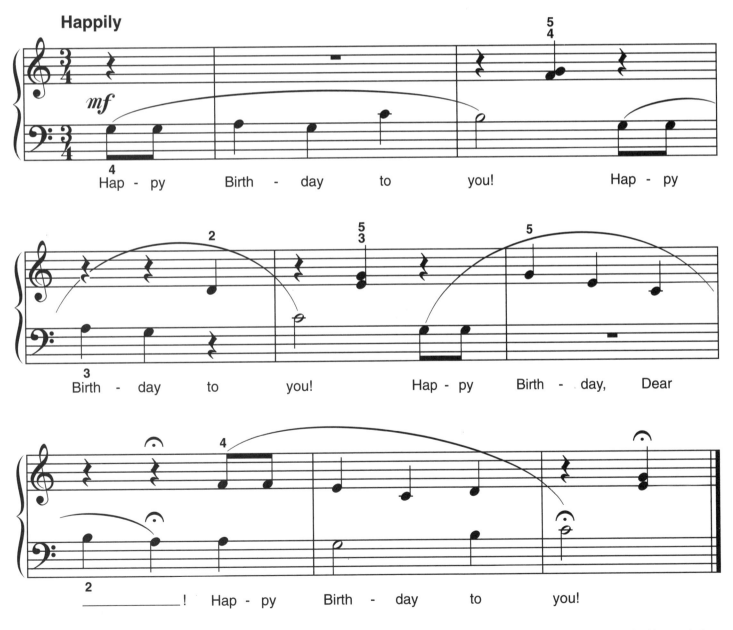

Hap - py   Birth - day   to   you!   Hap - py

Birth - day   to   you!   Hap - py   Birth - day,   Dear

_____ !   Hap - py   Birth - day   to   you!

More on Eighth Notes

This piece will prepare you to play EIGHTH NOTES.

1. Play at a very moderate speed. Count aloud, very evenly.
   The sign ⌒ over the G in the sixth measure is a FERMATA or "hold" sign. Hold the note longer than its value. (Approximately *twice* its value is a good general rule.)

2. Play again, saying or singing the words.

SHOO, FLY, SHOO! 🔊45

Counting Eighth Notes

Two eighth notes are played in the time of **one quarter note**.

To count music containing eighth notes, divide each beat into two parts:

count: **"1 - &"** or **"quar - ter"**
    for each quarter note;

count: **"1 - &"** or **"2 - 8ths"**
    for each pair of eighth notes.

COUNT: "1 - &, 1 - &," *etc.*
or: "quar- ter, 2 - 8ths," *etc.*

1. Play *SKIP TO MY LOU!* at the same speed you played *SHOO, FLY, SHOO!* Count aloud.

2. Play again, saying or singing the words.

SKIP TO MY LOU! 🔊46

STANDING IN THE NEED OF PRAYER

For this popular spiritual, we return to C POSITION (LH 5 on C).

Rhythmically, not too fast

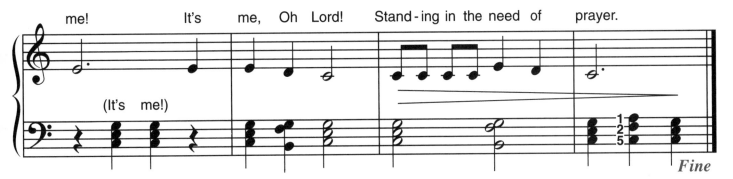

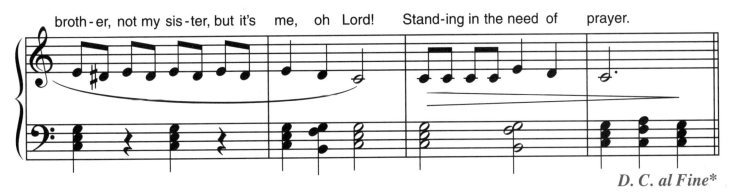

* **D. C. al Fine (Da Capo al Fine)** means *repeat from the beginning and play to the end (Fine)*.

THE AMAZING AEROBICS OF HANON

Charles-Louis Hanon (1819–1900) wrote, "The 4th and 5th fingers are almost useless because of the lack of special exercises to strengthen them." He then proceeded to devise some exercises which were so successful that they brought him worldwide fame. They are still used as warm-ups by the most skilled pianists of the present day.

No. 1 🔊

Skip the interval of a 3rd between LH 5 & 4 and between RH 1 & 2 on the first two notes of this exercise, then play up and down in 2nds. The LH 5 and RH 1 then fall on the note that was skipped in the first measure, and the hands move to a higher position in each following measure. After you reach the highest note of the exercise, descend by skipping a 3rd between RH 5 & 4, and between LH 1 & 2.

This remarkable exercise gives practice in stretching the LH 4th & 5th fingers while ascending, and the 4th & 5th fingers of the RH while descending.

The exercise is so simple to grasp that you do not even have to look at the music to play it, and you can continue up the keyboard as far as you wish.

LIFT FINGERS HIGH and play each note distinctly. Practice slowly at first, then gradually increase speed.

Moderately slow to Moderately fast

No. 2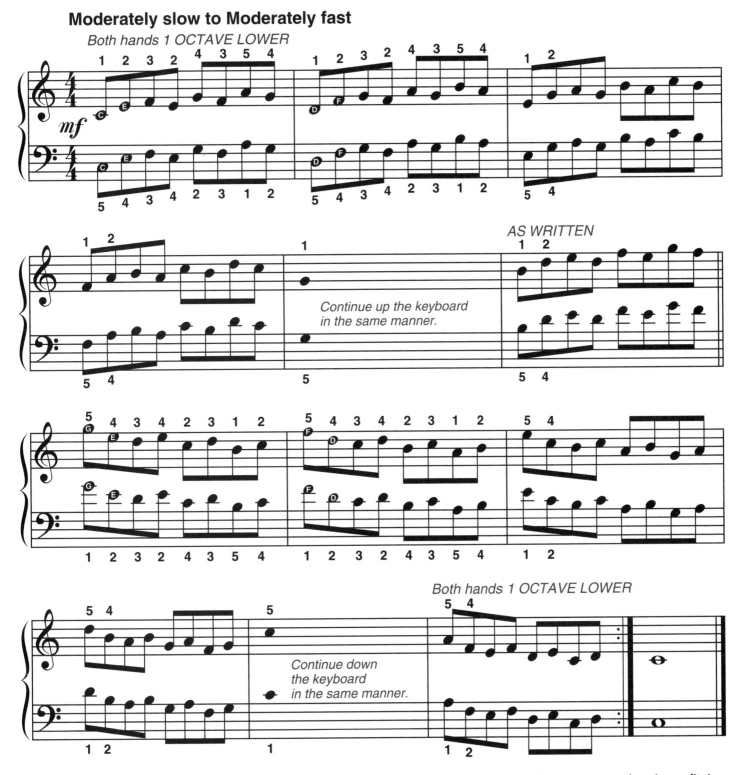

This exercise is chosen from the HANON series because it uses the same system as the previous one for moving up and down the keyboard, and because it not only continues the stretch between the 5th and 4th fingers but also strengthens the remaining fingers equally.

Once you have grasped the pattern of the exercise, you will not have to look at the music to play it. Continue up the keyboard as far as you wish.

LIFT FINGERS HIGH and play each note distinctly. Practice slowly at first, then gradually increase speed.

Moderately slow to Moderately fast

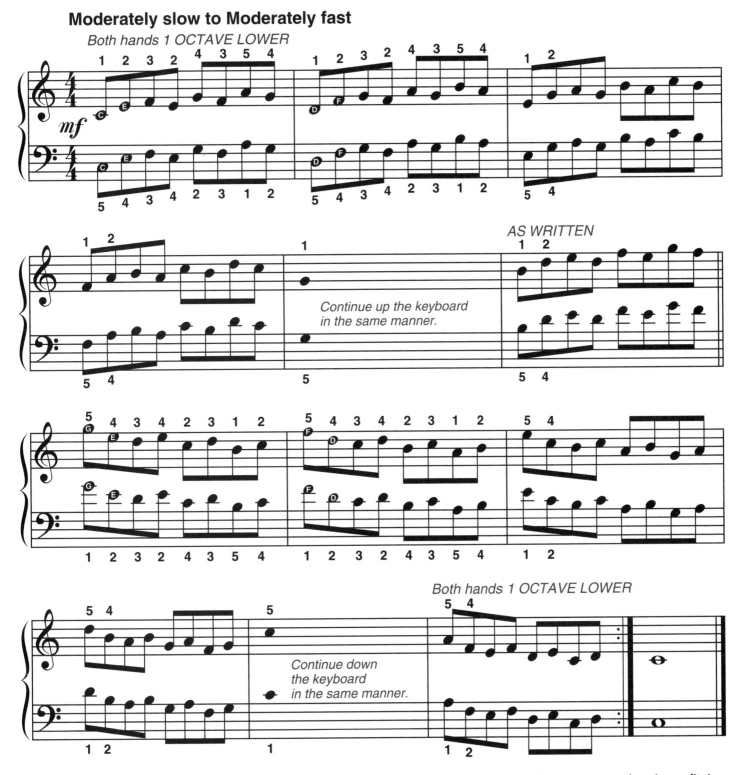

After you have learned to play Nos. 1 & 2 evenly, at a moderate speed, you may also benefit by practicing them softly, with the fingers close to the keys. On the repeat, play very loudly, lifting the fingers very high. It is also good to begin each exercise softly, making a gradual crescendo as you go higher, then gradually diminuendo as you come down again to the lowest notes. This builds great control of each finger muscle.

Introducing Dotted Quarter Notes

A DOT INCREASES THE LENGTH OF A NOTE BY ONE HALF ITS VALUE.

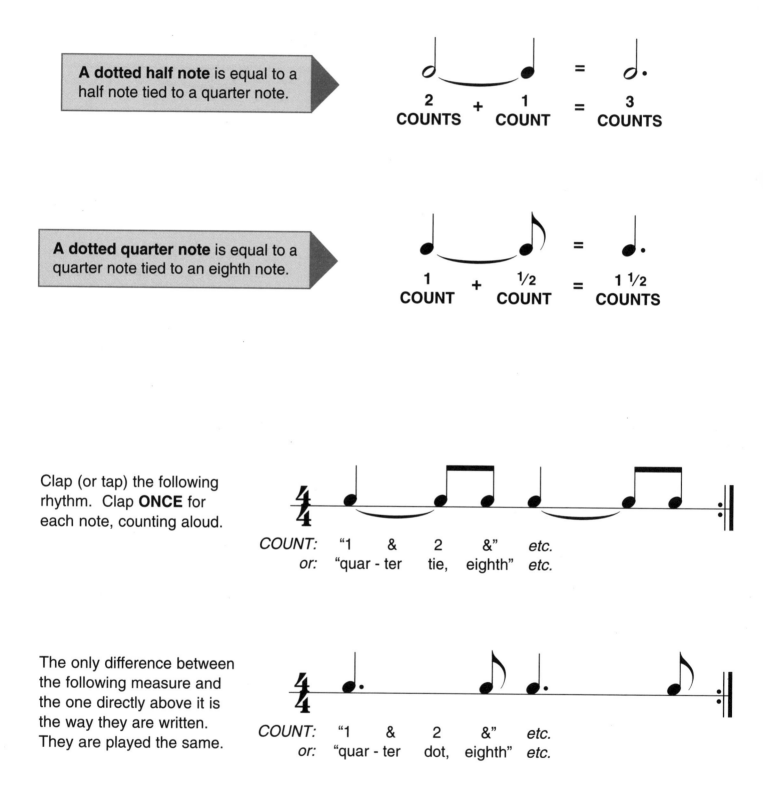

A dotted half note is equal to a half note tied to a quarter note.

A dotted quarter note is equal to a quarter note tied to an eighth note.

Clap (or tap) the following rhythm. Clap **ONCE** for each note, counting aloud.

The only difference between the following measure and the one directly above it is the way they are written. They are played the same.

In 4/4 or 3/4 time, the DOTTED QUARTER NOTE is almost *always* followed by an EIGHTH NOTE!

MEASURES FROM FAMILIAR SONGS USING DOTTED QUARTER NOTES

1. Count & clap (or tap) the notes.   2. Play & count.   3. Play & sing the words.

C POSITION

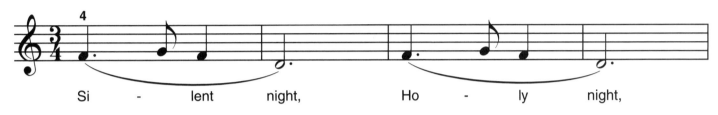

MIDDLE C POSITION (Both thumbs on Middle C)

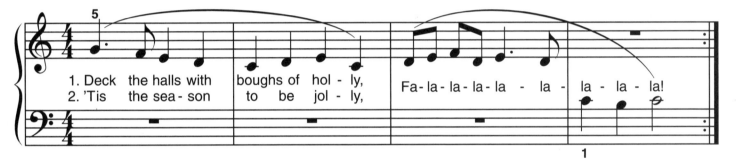

MIDDLE C POSITION

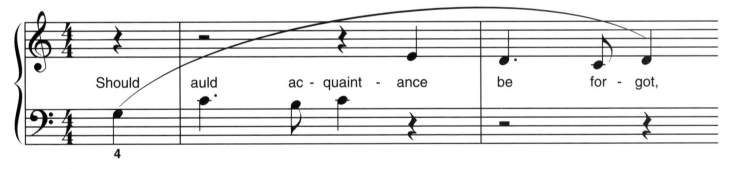

C POSITION

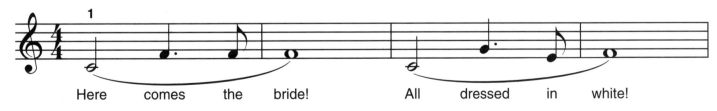

ALOUETTE 🔊

C POSITION

Brightly

French folk song

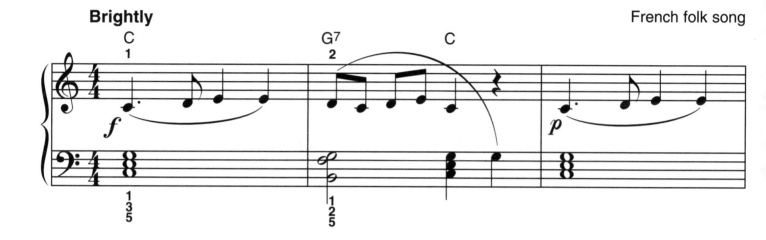

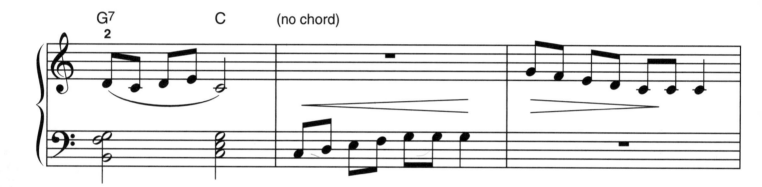

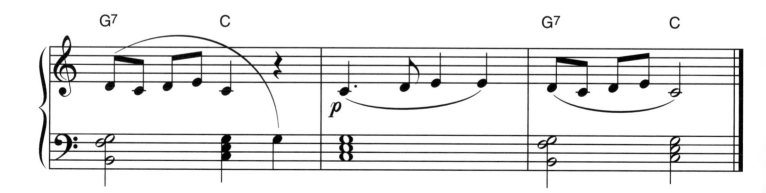

Measuring 6ths

When you skip 4 white keys, the interval is a **6th.**

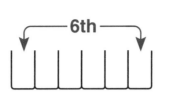

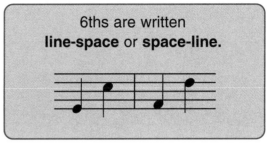

6ths are written **line-space** or **space-line.**

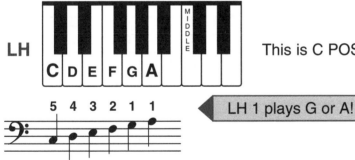

RH

This is C POSITION plus one note (A) played with 5.

RH 5 plays G or A!

Say the names of these intervals as you play!

MELODIC INTERVALS

2nd   3rd   4th   5th   6th

HARMONIC INTERVALS

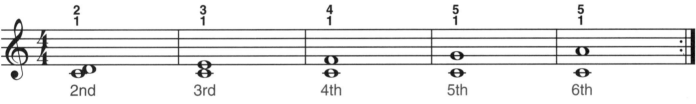

2nd   3rd   4th   5th   6th

LH

This is C POSITION plus one note (A) played with 1.

LH 1 plays G or A!

Say the names of these intervals as you play!

MELODIC INTERVALS

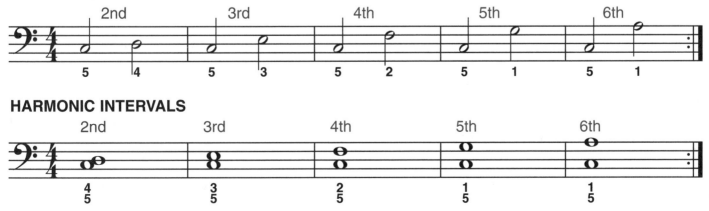

HARMONIC INTERVALS

In *LAVENDER'S BLUE,* 5ths and 6ths are played with 1 & 5.
Practice this warm-up before playing *LAVENDER'S BLUE.*

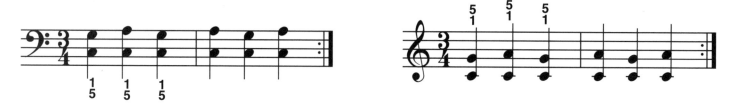

LAVENDER'S BLUE

C POSITION + 1

Moderately fast

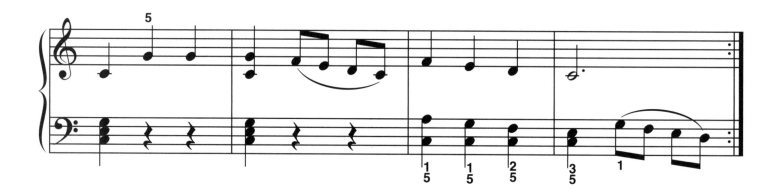

ritardando means gradually slowing.

KUM-BA-YAH!*

WITH CHANGING TIME SIGNATURES

NEW TIME SIGNATURE

2 means **2** beats to each measure.

4 means a **QUARTER NOTE** ♩ gets one beat.

Moderately slow

2nd time both hands 8va

1. Kum - ba - yah,   my Lord,   Kum - ba - yah!
2. Some - one's   pray - ing, Lord,   Kum - ba - yah!

COUNT: 1 & 2 &   1 & 2 & 3 & 4 &

Kum - ba - yah,   my Lord,   Kum - ba - yah!
Some - one's   pray - ing, Lord,   Kum - ba - yah!

Kum - ba - yah,   my Lord,   Kum - ba - yah!
Some - one's   pray - ing, Lord,   Kum - ba - yah!

Oh,   Lord,   Kum - ba - yah!
Oh,   Lord,   Kum - ba - yah!

Kum-ba-yah means "Come by here."

Writing 6ths

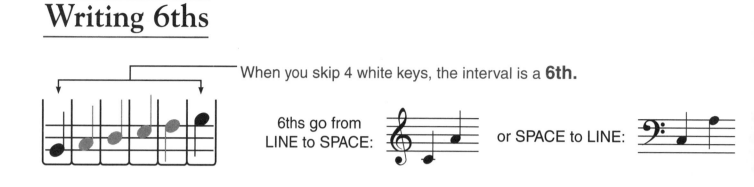

When you skip 4 white keys, the interval is a **6th.**

6ths go from LINE to SPACE: or SPACE to LINE:

1. Write the names of the keys a 6th apart on this keyboard, beginning with the lowest C:

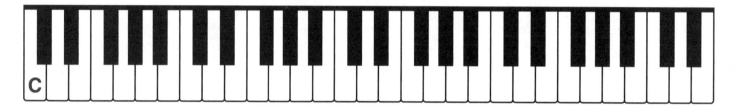

C

2. Write the names of these MELODIC intervals in the boxes.

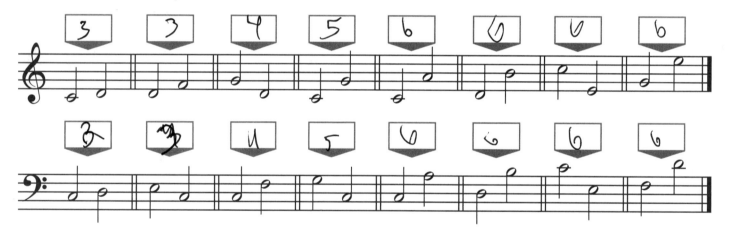

3. Write the names of these HARMONIC intervals in the boxes.

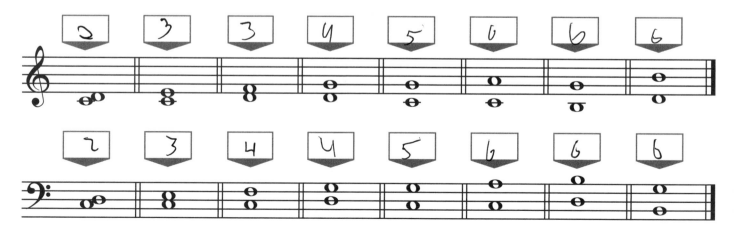

HANON'S AEROBIC SIXTHS 🔊

This exercise will make you thoroughly familiar with the interval of a 6th, at the same time giving all fingers a great workout!

Notice how cleverly Hanon uses the 6th to raise the hands to the next higher position, then to lower them back again.

LIFT FINGERS HIGH. Play each note clearly and distinctly. Practice slowly, then gradually increase speed.

Moderately slow to Moderately fast

More exercises by Hanon may be found in Alfred publication No. 617, *Hanon, Book 1;* or No. 616, *Hanon, The Virtuoso Pianist in 60 Exercises (Complete Edition).*

When you play in positions that include six or more notes,
any finger may be required to play two notes.

LONDON BRIDGE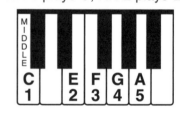

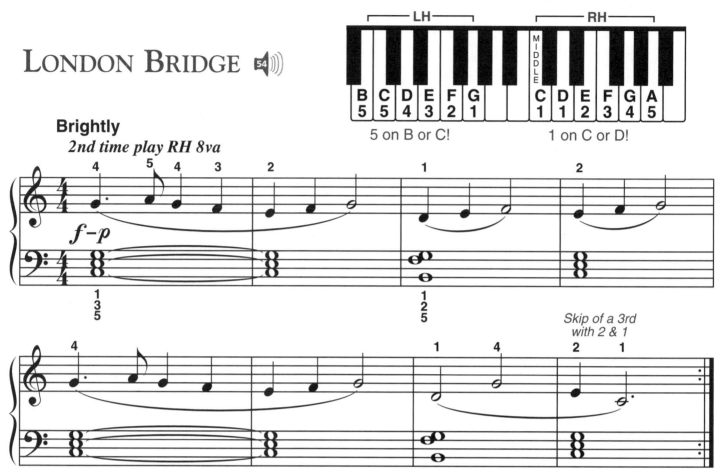

5 on B or C!   1 on C or D!

Brightly
2nd time play RH 8va

f–p

*Skip of a 3rd
with 2 & 1*

RH 1 plays C, RH 2 plays E.

MICHAEL, ROW THE BOAT ASHORE

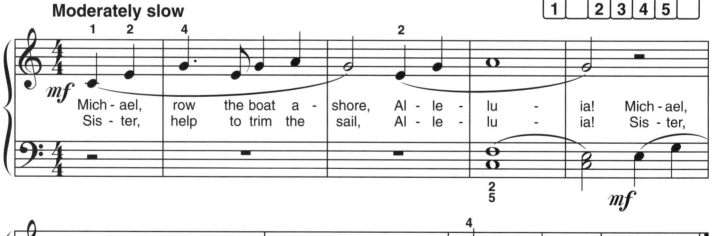

Moderately slow

mf

Mich - ael, row the boat a - shore, Al - le - lu - ia! Mich - ael,
Sis - ter, help to trim the sail, Al - le - lu - ia! Sis - ter,

mf

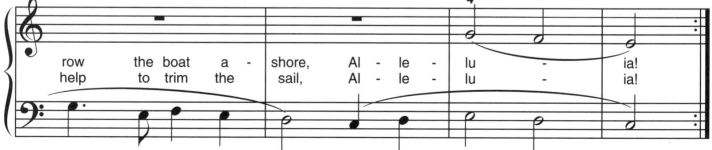

row the boat a - shore, Al - le - lu - ia!
help to trim the sail, Al - le - lu - ia!

BLOW THE MAN DOWN!

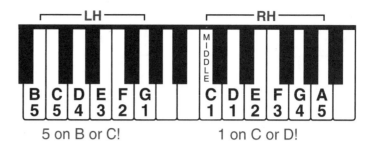

5 on B or C!   1 on C or D!

Moderately fast

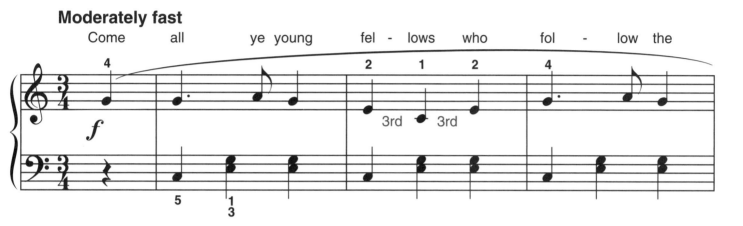

Come all ye young fel - lows who fol - low the

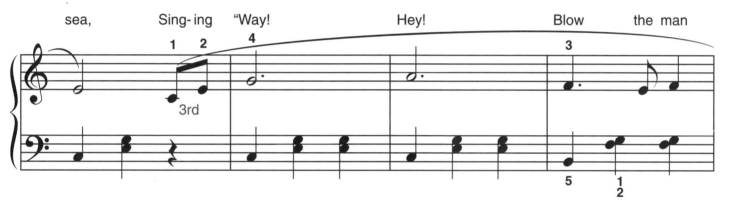

sea, Sing- ing "Way! Hey! Blow the man

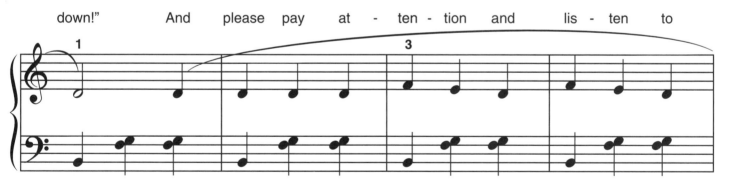

down!" And please pay at - ten - tion and lis - ten to

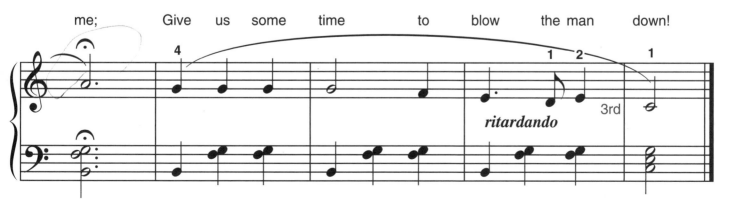

me; Give us some time to blow the man down!

Moving Up & Down the Keyboard in 6ths

To play popular and classical music, you must be able to move freely over the keyboard. These exercises will prepare you to do this. Each hand plays 6ths, moving up and down the keyboard to neighboring keys. READ ONLY THE LOWEST NOTE OF EACH INTERVAL, adding a 6th above!

RH 6ths, MOVING FROM A/C **UP TO** E/G **AND BACK.**

Begin with RH 1 on MIDDLE C.

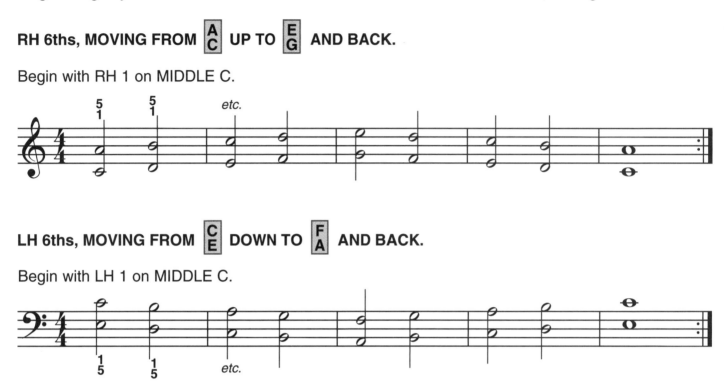

LH 6ths, MOVING FROM C/E **DOWN TO** F/A **AND BACK.**

Begin with LH 1 on MIDDLE C.

LONE STAR WALTZ 57

This piece combines the positions used in *LONDON BRIDGE* with *Moving Up & Down the Keyboard in 6ths.*

Moderate waltz tempo
2nd time both hands 8va

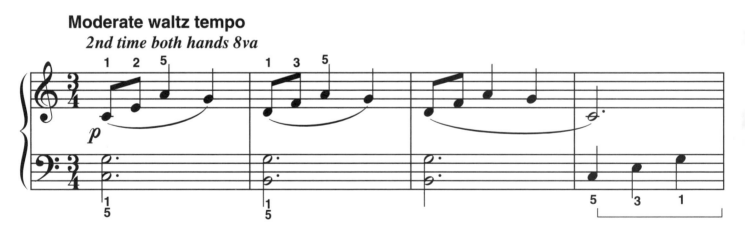

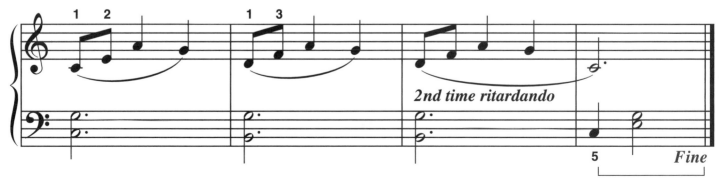

2nd time ritardando

Fine

The dot over or under the notes indicates the **STACCATO** touch. Make these notes very short!

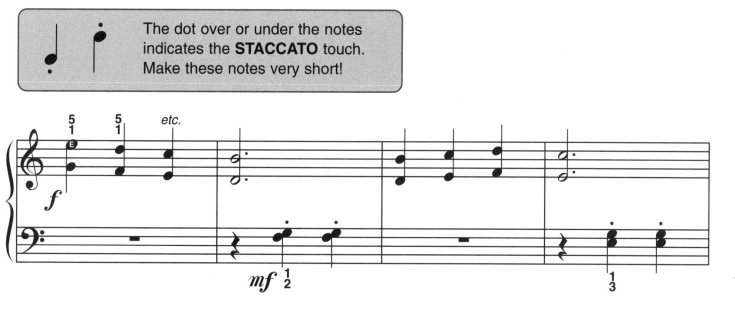

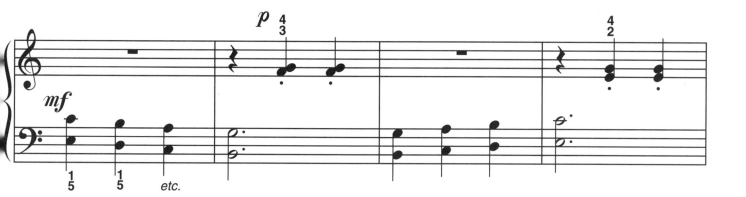

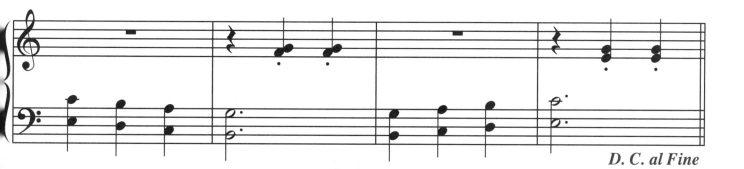

D. C. al Fine

Measuring 7ths & Octaves

When you skip 5 white keys,
the interval is a **7th.**

When you skip 6 white keys,
the interval is an **OCTAVE.**

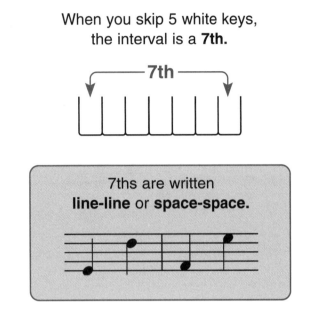

7ths are written
line-line or **space-space.**

OCTAVES are written
line-space or **space-line.**

Say the names of these intervals as you play!

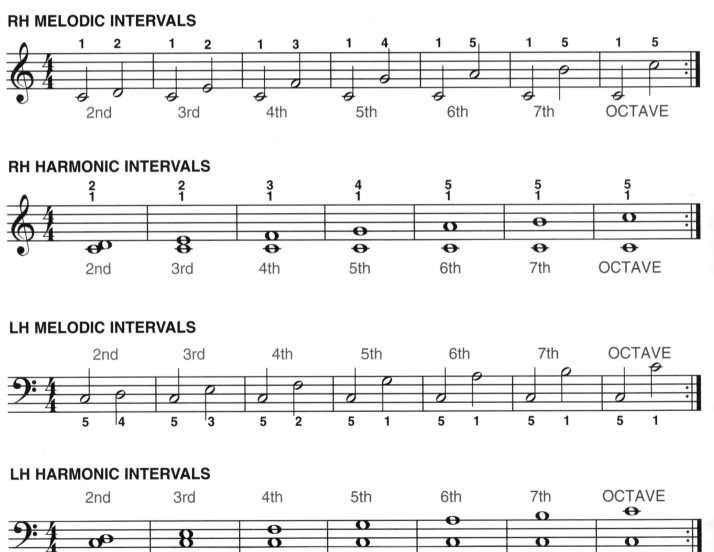

RH MELODIC INTERVALS

2nd 3rd 4th 5th 6th 7th OCTAVE

RH HARMONIC INTERVALS

2nd 3rd 4th 5th 6th 7th OCTAVE

LH MELODIC INTERVALS

2nd 3rd 4th 5th 6th 7th OCTAVE

LH HARMONIC INTERVALS

2nd 3rd 4th 5th 6th 7th OCTAVE

Writing 7ths & Octaves

When you skip 5 white keys, the interval is a **7th.**

7ths are written
LINE–LINE: or SPACE–SPACE:

When you skip 6 white keys, the interval is an **OCTAVE.**

OCTAVES are written
LINE–SPACE: or SPACE–LINE:

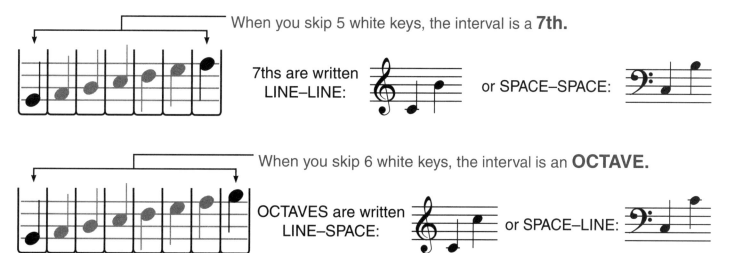

1. In each measure below, add a higher half note to make the indicated MELODIC interval.
2. Play. Use RH 1–5 or LH 5–1 on the 5th, 6th, 7th & OCTAVE.

| 2nd | 3rd | 4th | 5th | 6th | 7th | octave |

| 2nd | 3rd | 4th | 5th | 6th | 7th | octave |

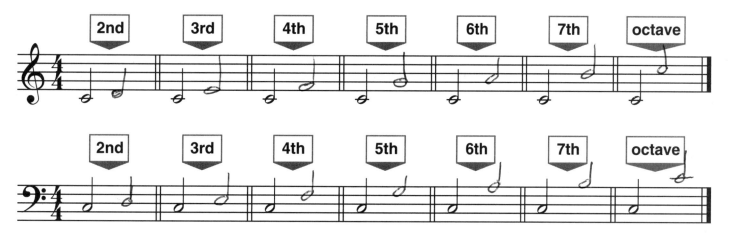

3. In each measure below, add a WHOLE NOTE directly above the given note
   to make the indicated HARMONIC interval.
4. Play. Use RH 1–5 or LH 5–1 on each interval.

| 7th | octave | 7th | octave | 7th | octave | octave | octave |

| octave | 7th | 7th | octave | octave | octave | 7th | 7th |

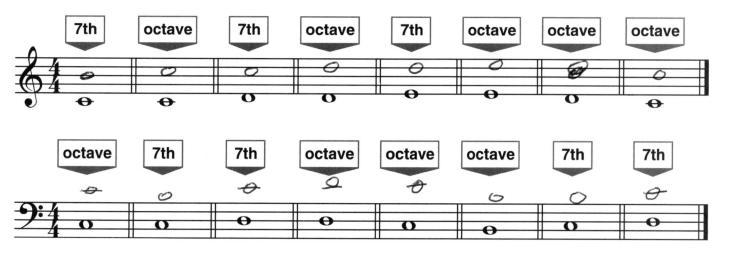

CAFÉ VIENNA 🔊))

Play hands separately at first, then together.

Be especially careful of the RH fingering!

Notice that the first two notes, a melodic 3rd, are played with 2 & 1!

Moderate waltz tempo

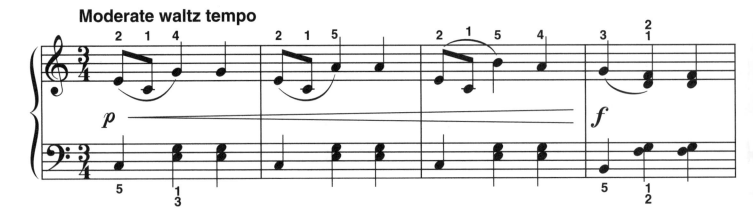

Lullaby

Johannes Brahms

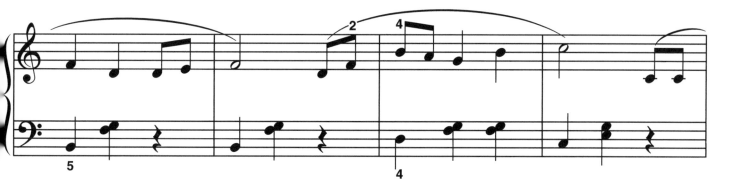

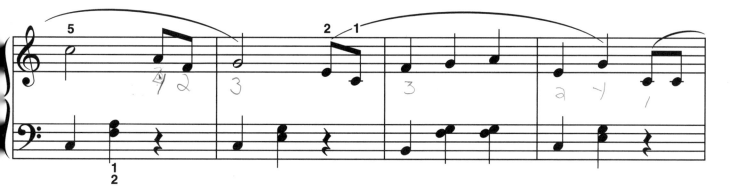

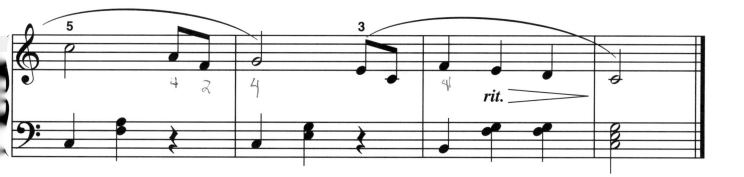

The Flat Sign

The **FLAT SIGN** before a note means play the next key to the LEFT, whether black or white!

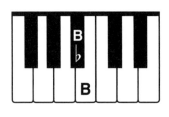

When a FLAT (♭) appears before a note, it applies to that note for the rest of the measure.

Circle the notes that are FLAT:

ROCK IT AWAY! 🔊

Moderately fast

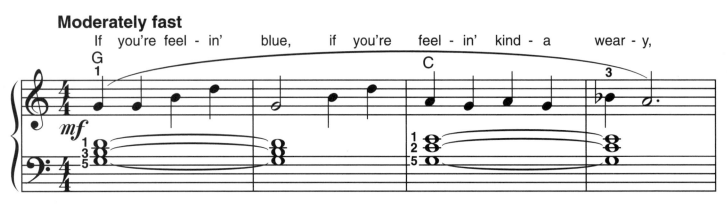

If you're feel - in' blue, if you're feel - in' kind - a wear - y,

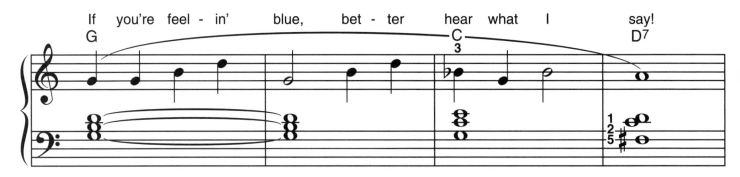

If you're feel - in' blue, bet - ter hear what I say!

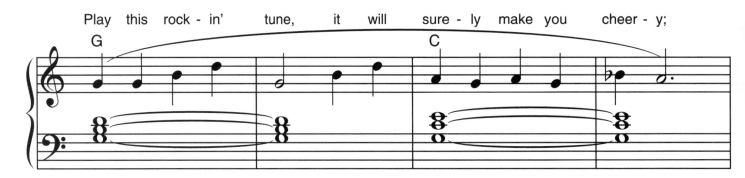

Play this rock - in' tune, it will sure - ly make you cheer - y;

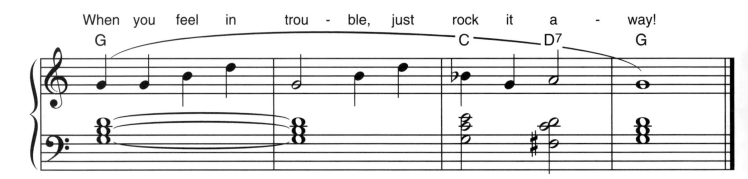

When you feel in trou - ble, just rock it a - way!

Writing the Flat Sign

1. Make some FLAT SIGNS:

First, draw one vertical line.

Then, add the heavier curved line.

Draw 4 flat signs here:

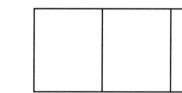

2. Write the names of the ♭ keys in the boxes below.

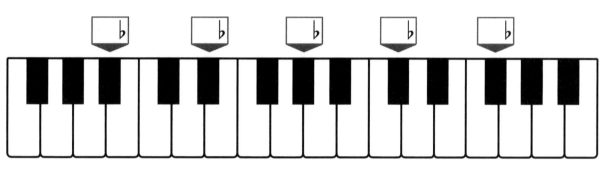

3. Change each of the notes below to a flat note. Write the flat sign BEFORE the note!

When writing flat signs, be sure to **CENTER** the flat sign on the line or space of the note to be flatted:

4. Write the name of each note in the box above it.

5. Play the notes, using RH 3 or LH 3.

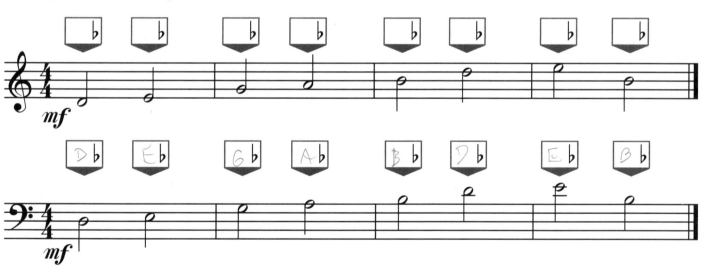

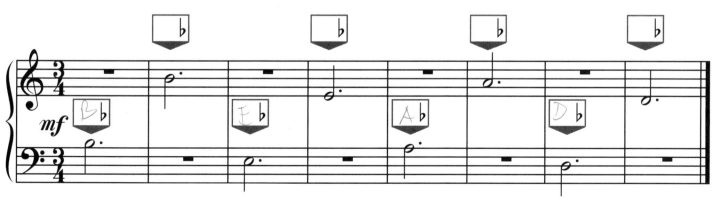

Measuring Half Steps & Whole Steps

HALF STEPS • NO KEY BETWEEN

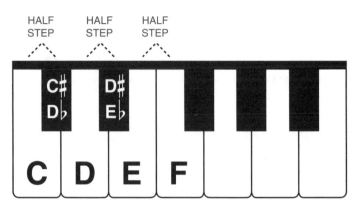

Half Steps

A **HALF STEP** is the distance from any key to the very next key above or below (black or white).

WHOLE STEPS • ONE KEY BETWEEN

Whole Steps

A **WHOLE STEP** is equal to 2 half steps. Skip one key (black or white).

Tetrachords

A **TETRACHORD** is a series of FOUR NOTES having a pattern of

WHOLE STEP, WHOLE STEP, HALF STEP.

The notes of a tetrachord must be in alphabetical order →

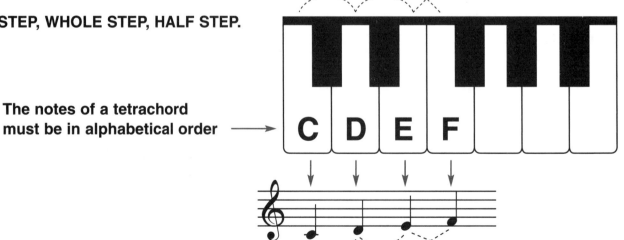

and must also have this pattern! →

Writing Half Steps & Whole Steps

1. In the following squares write $\frac{1}{2}$ for each HALF STEP and 1 for each WHOLE STEP indicated by the arrows.

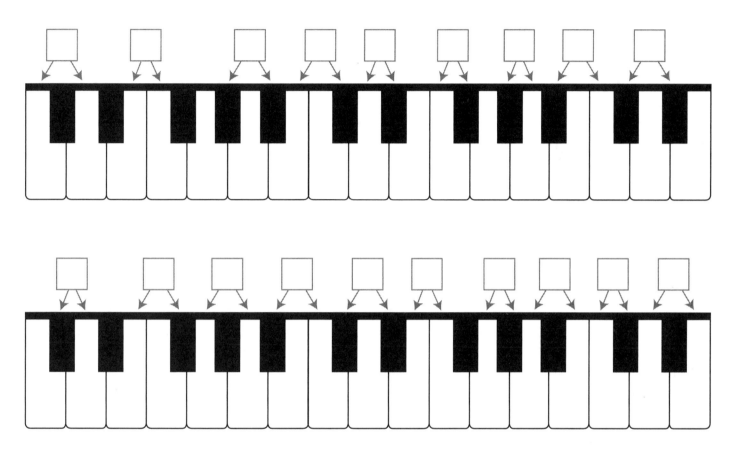

Tetrachords

2. Study the TETRACHORDS below and answer these questions:

• Does each consist of WHOLE STEP, WHOLE STEP, HALF STEP? Answer: _____

• Are the notes of each tetrachord NEIGHBORING LETTERS of the musical alphabet?
  Answer: _____

• Underline the correct spelling of the **D** tetrachord: **D E G♭ G**   **D E F♯ G**

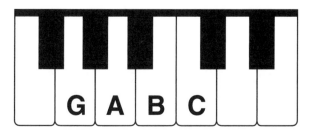

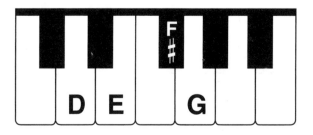

The Major Scale

The MAJOR SCALE is made of **TWO TETRACHORDS** *joined* by a **WHOLE STEP**.

The C MAJOR SCALE is constructed as follows:

There is no ♯ or ♭
in the **C MAJOR SCALE.**

Each scale begins and ends on a note of the same name as the scale, called the **KEY NOTE.**

Preparation for Scale Playing

IMPORTANT!   Since there are **8** notes in the C major scale and we only have **5** fingers,
an important trick must be mastered: **passing the thumb under the 3rd finger!**
This exercise will make this trick easy.

Play HANDS SEPARATELY. Begin VERY SLOWLY. Keep the wrist loose and quiet!

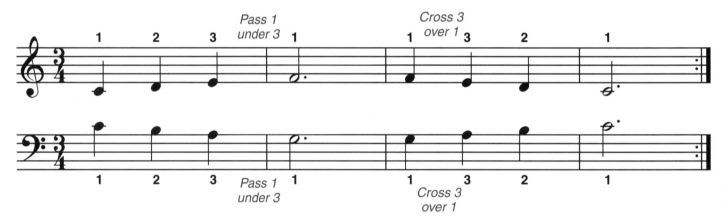

The C Major Scale

Begin SLOWLY. *Lean* the hand slightly in the direction you are moving.
The hand should move smoothly along, with no twisting motion of the wrist!

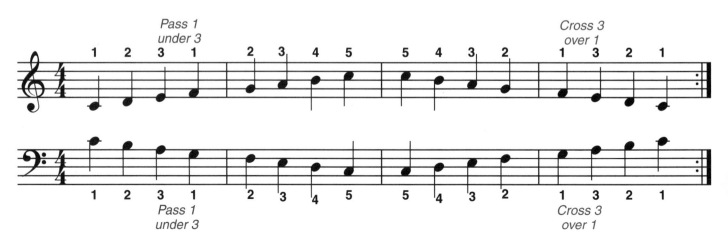

Writing the Major Scale

1. Write the letter names of the notes of the C MAJOR SCALE, from left to right, on the keyboard below. Use the tetrachord patterns, and be sure each whole step and half step is correct!

THE C MAJOR SCALE

2. Complete the tetrachord beginning on C. Write one note over each finger number.

3. Complete the tetrachord beginning on G. Write one note under each finger number.

4. Play the above. Use LH on the first tetrachord and RH on the second tetrachord.

5. Complete a tetrachord beginning on each of the notes below. Write one note under each finger number.

6. Play with RH. By crossing 1 under 3, you can play the entire scale of 8 notes with the 5 fingers of one hand!

7. Complete a tetrachord beginning on each of the notes below. Write one note over each finger number.

8. Play with LH. Cross 3 over 1.

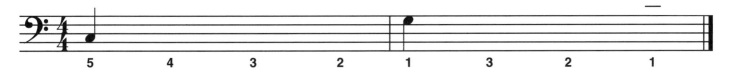

9. Play each of the above two scales again, beginning on the HIGHEST note, and descending to the LOWEST. (Read the notes and fingering in REVERSE, from right to left!) Play the first with RH, crossing 3 over 1, and the second with LH, passing 1 under 3.

These Hands Were Made for Playing

The fact that the thumb opposes the remaining fingers is one of the significant differences between humans and animals. It enables us to use tools skillfully, to write and paint, and also to make music. It is a particularly important factor in playing a keyboard instrument.

The musculature of the hand allows the thumb to pivot under the palm of the hand and easily touch the base of the 4th finger. By making use of this facility, we have the ability to move the thumb to play a key, and then we can shift the position of the hand. This enables us to play continuously up or down the entire piano keyboard.

The following drawings are views of the PALM of the hand.

The drawing on the left shows the *palmar fascia,* the connective tissue that supports the muscles of the inner part of the hand.

The drawing on the right shows how the thumb reaches under to the base of the 4th finger to play scales of eight or more notes without interrupting the flow of the notes.

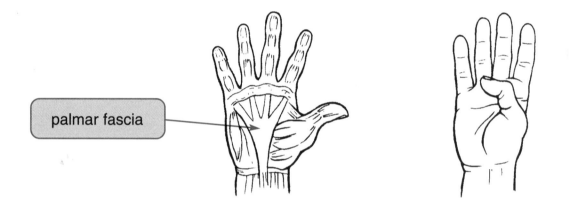

palmar fascia

PLAYING THE C MAJOR SCALE

As soon as the thumb has played the first note (while the 2nd finger is playing the second note), pass the thumb under to the base of the 4th finger, so it will be ready to play its next note in advance.

This is one of the most important secrets of smooth, legato scale playing!

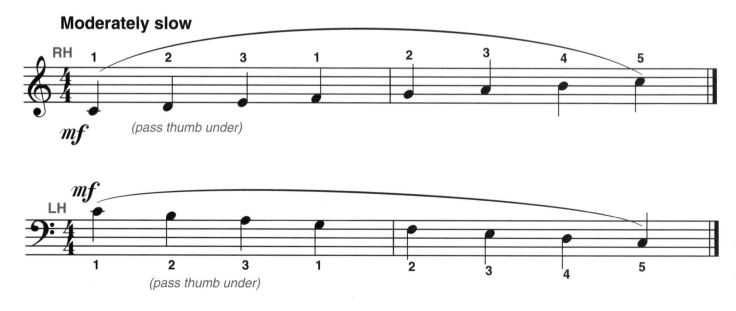

JOY TO THE WORLD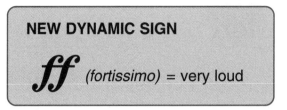

Scales occur often in melodies. This favorite melody is made up almost entirely of major scales.

George Frideric Handel

Joyfully

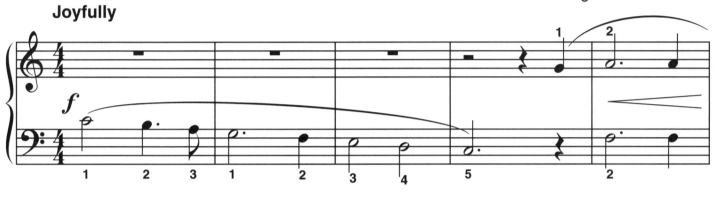

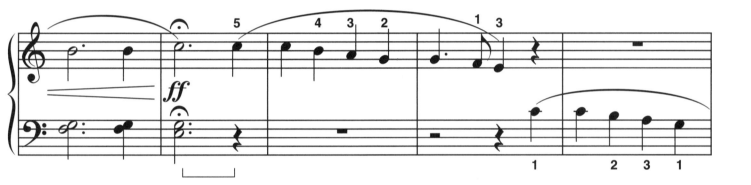

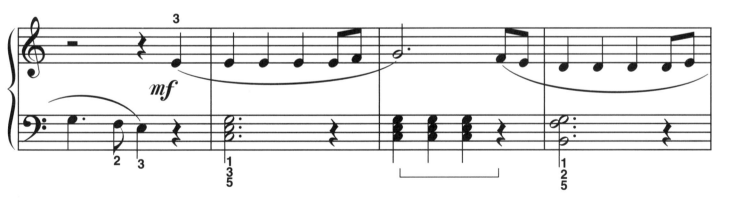

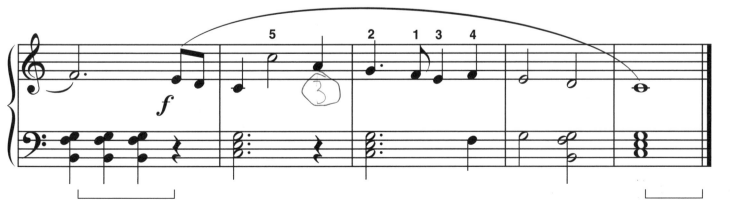

More About Chords

A TRIAD IS A 3-NOTE CHORD.

The three notes of a triad are:

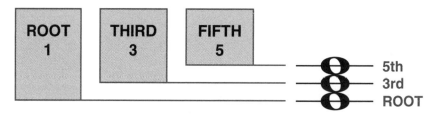

| ROOT | THIRD | FIFTH |
| 1 | 3 | 5 |

5th
3rd
ROOT

The ROOT is the note from which the triad gets its name. The root of a C triad is C.

Triads in **ROOT POSITION** (with root at the bottom) always look like this:

LINE — 5th
LINE — 3rd
LINE — ROOT

or this:

SPACE — 5th
SPACE — 3rd
SPACE — ROOT

> **Triads may be built on any note of any scale.**

TRIADS BUILT ON THE C MAJOR SCALE

Play with RH:

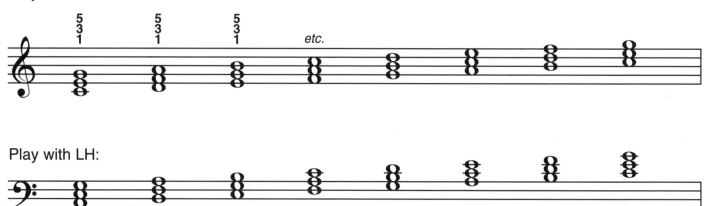

Play with LH:

Listen carefully to the sound of these root-position triads!

When you name the notes of any **TRIAD IN ROOT POSITION,** you will always skip **ONE** letter of the musical alphabet between each note. The triads you played above are:

C E G   D F A   E G B   F A C   G B D   A C E   B D F

This is the complete **"TRIAD VOCABULARY."** It should be memorized!

COCKLES AND MUSSELS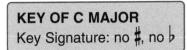

KEY OF C MAJOR
Key Signature: no #, no ♭

Music based on any particular scale is said to be in the **KEY** of that scale.
If there are sharps or flats in the scale, they are shown at the beginning of the music. This is called the **KEY SIGNATURE.**

Moderately slow

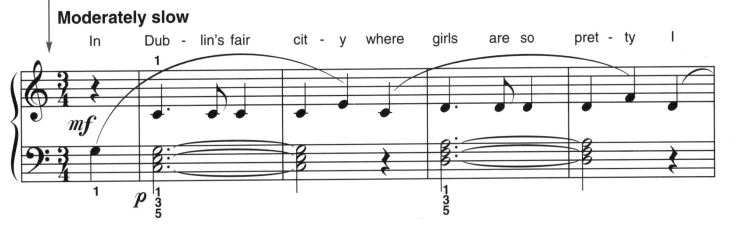

In Dub - lin's fair cit - y where girls are so pret - ty I

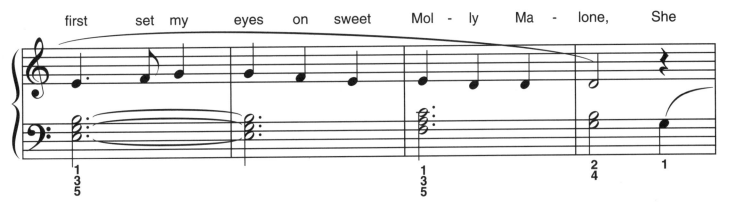

first set my eyes on sweet Mol - ly Ma - lone, She

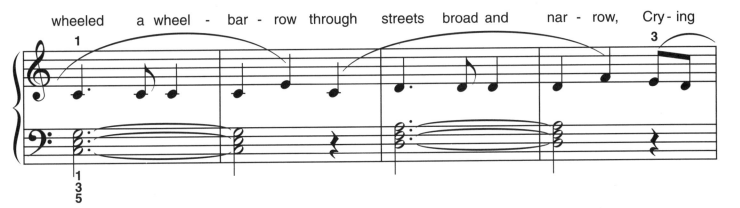

wheeled a wheel - bar - row through streets broad and nar - row, Cry - ing

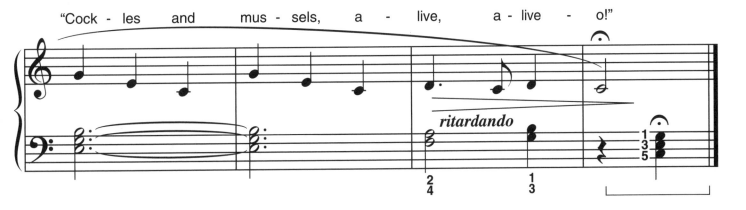

"Cock - les and mus - sels, a - live, a - live - o!"

ritardando

The Primary Chords in C Major

The three most important chords in any key are those built on the 1st, 4th & 5th notes of the scale. These are called the **PRIMARY CHORDS** of the key.

The chords are identified by the Roman numerals **I, IV & V** (1, 4 & 5).

The **V** chord usually adds the note a 7th above the root to make a V^7 (say "5-7") chord.

In the key of C major, the **I CHORD** is the C MAJOR TRIAD.

The **IV CHORD** is the F MAJOR TRIAD.

The V^7 **CHORD** is the G^7 CHORD (G major triad with an added 7th).

The Primary Chords in C Major

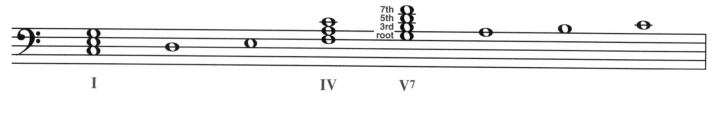

Chord Progressions

When we change from one chord to another, we call this a **CHORD PROGRESSION.**

When all chords are in root position, the hand must leap from one chord to the next. To make the chord progressions easier to play and sound better, the **IV** and V^7 chords may be played in other positions by moving one or more of the higher chord tones down an octave.

The **I** chord is played in ROOT POSITION:

The top note of the **IV** chord is moved down an octave:

In the V^7 chord, the 5th (D) is usually omitted. All notes except the root are moved down an octave:

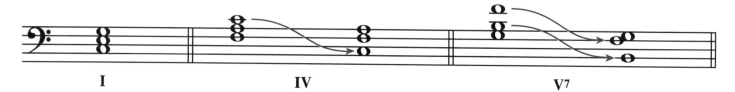

The three PRIMARY CHORDS are then comfortably played as follows:

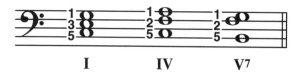

It is important that you now think of the C, F & G^7 chords in the key of C MAJOR as the **I, IV & V^7** chords!

Play the following line several times, saying the numerals of each chord as you play.

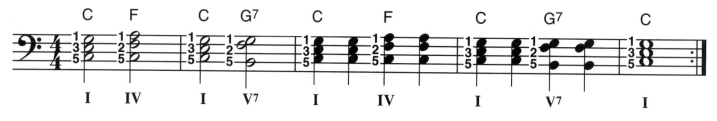

About the Blues

Music called **BLUES** has long been a part of the American musical heritage. We find it in the music of many popular songwriters, in ballads, boogie, and rock.

BLUES music follows a basic formula, that is, a standard chord progression. If you learn the formula for *GOT THOSE BLUES!* you will be able to play the blues in any key you learn, simply by applying the formula to that key.

Formula for the Blues

There are 12 measures in one chorus of the blues:

4 measures of the **I** chord
2 measures of the **IV** chord
2 measures of the **I** chord
1 measure of the **V^7** chord
1 measure of the **IV** chord
2 measures of the **I** chord

GOT THOSE BLUES! 63

*The eighth notes may be played a bit unevenly:

long   short   long   short, *etc.*

Chords and the Blues Progression

THREE IMPORTANT CHORDS
USED IN JAZZ/ROCK:

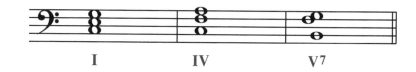

CREATING A BLUES PROGRESSION

The blues progression is a series of chords
which usually uses the **I**, **IV**, **V⁷** chords
and is generally 12 measures long.

> The **NATURAL SIGN** cancels
> a sharp or flat!
>
> A note after a natural sign
> is always a *white key!*

THE C MAJOR BLUES PROGRESSION

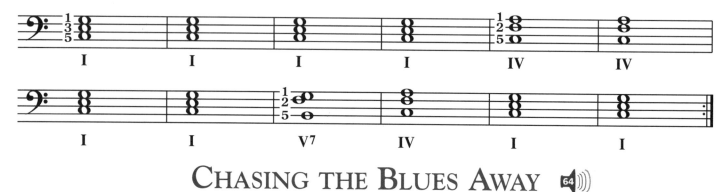

CHASING THE BLUES AWAY 🔊

Now we add a melody to the C Blues Progression and call it the *blues.*

Slowly

Bert Konowitz

This and the next page are from Alfred's Jazz/Rock Adult Course (#3134) by Bert Konowitz.

BLUES FOR WYNTON MARSALIS

Wynton Marsalis is a great jazz trumpet player. He grew up in New Orleans, a city known for great blues. Wynton plays the blues with jazz groups, as well as classical music with the world's finest symphony orchestras.

Playing the right-hand eighth notes in a Jazz style
will sound perfect with the Walking Blue Note bass.

INTRODUCTION

Bert Konowitz

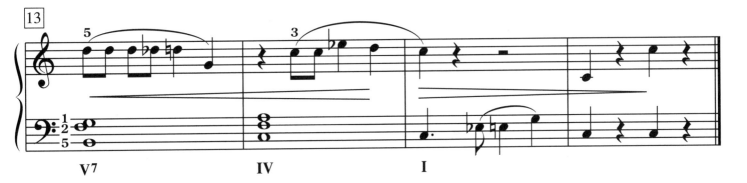

RH: An Extended Position

ON TOP OF OLD SMOKY begins and ends with the RH in an EXTENDED POSITION.

Play several times:

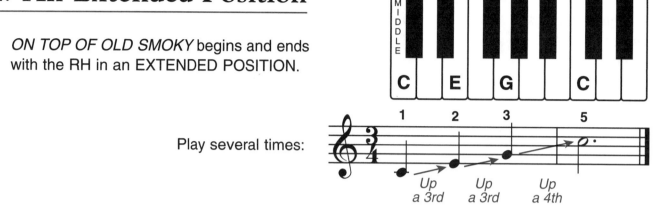

LH Review: Block Chords & Broken Chords in C

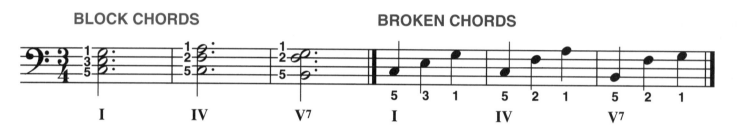

ON TOP OF OLD SMOKY 🔊

KEY OF C MAJOR
Key Signature: no ♯, no ♭

Moderately slow

EXTENDED POSITION

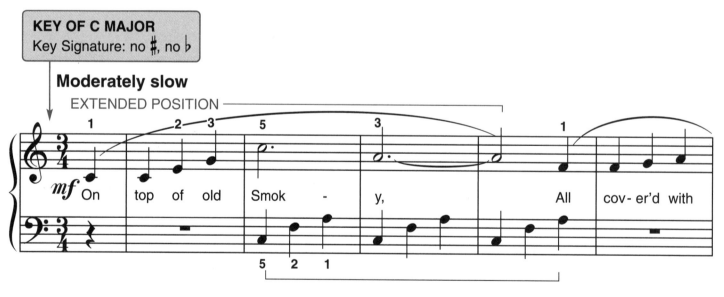

mf On top of old Smok - y, All cov-er'd with

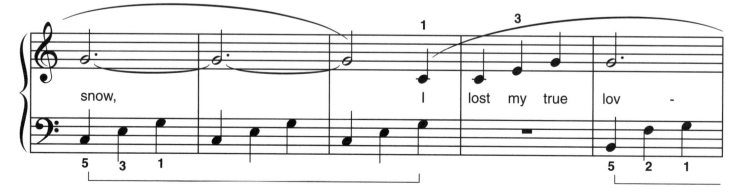

snow, I lost my true lov -

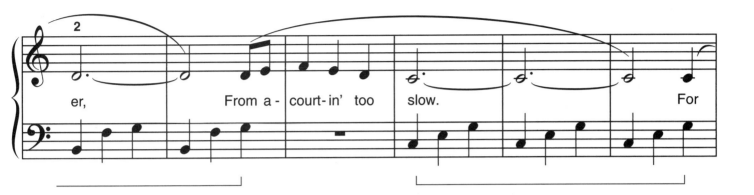

er, From a - court-in' too slow. For

court - in's a pleas - ure, And part - in' is

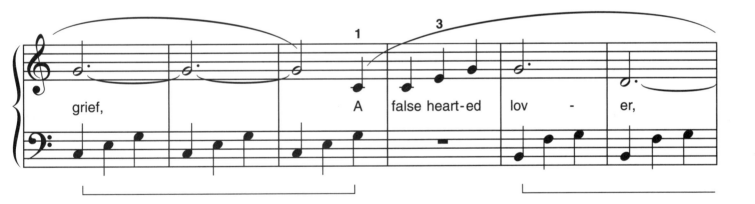

grief, A false heart-ed lov - er,

Is worse than a thief.

The G Major Scale

Remember that the MAJOR SCALE is made up of two tetrachords *joined* by a whole step.
The second TETRACHORD of the G MAJOR SCALE begins on D.

There is 1 sharp (F♯)
in the **G MAJOR SCALE.**

The Key of G Major

A piece based on the G major scale is in the **KEY OF G MAJOR.**
Since F is sharp in the G scale, every F will be sharp in the key of G major.

Instead of placing a sharp before every F in the entire piece,
the sharp is indicated at the beginning in the KEY SIGNATURE.

KEY OF G MAJOR
Key Signature: 1 sharp (F♯)
Play all F's sharp throughout.

Practice the G major scale with HANDS SEPARATE.
Begin SLOWLY. Keep the wrist loose and quiet.

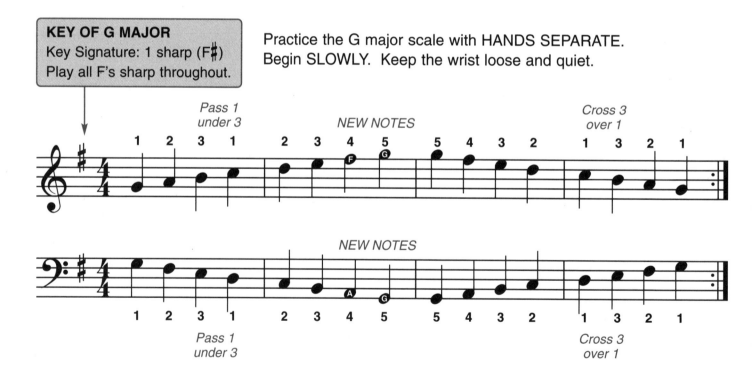

IMPORTANT! After you have learned the G MAJOR SCALE with hands separate, you may play the hands together. When the scale is played as written on the staffs above, the LH descends as the RH ascends, and vice versa. This is called CONTRARY MOTION—both hands play the *same numbered* fingers at the same time!

You may also play the C MAJOR SCALE at the bottom of page 100 with the hands together, in CONTRARY MOTION!

A New Trick!

CHANGING FINGERS ON THE SAME NOTE: Sometimes it is necessary to replay the same note with a different finger. Practice the following line to prepare for *THE CAN-CAN.*

THE CAN-CAN

KEY OF G MAJOR
Key Signature: 1 sharp (F♯)

Jacques Offenbach

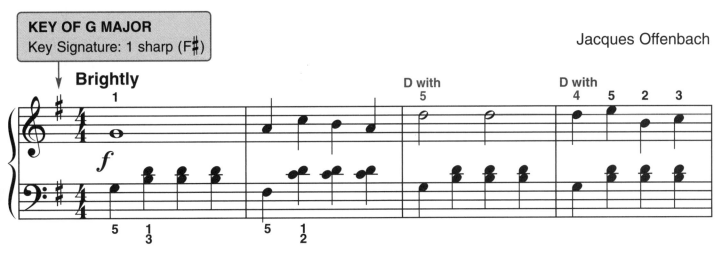

*Descending G major scale

Writing in the Key of G Major

1. Write the letter names of the notes of the G MAJOR SCALE on the keyboard below.
   Use the tetrachord patterns, and be sure each whole step and half step is correct!

THE G MAJOR SCALE

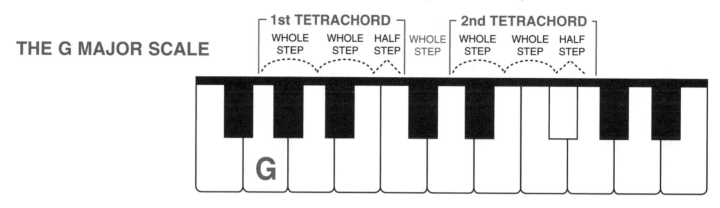

Check to be sure that you named the notes in the order of the musical alphabet. If you did, the black key will be named as a *sharp,* not a *flat!*

2. Complete the tetrachord beginning on G.
   Write one note over each finger number.

3. Complete the tetrachord beginning on D.
   Write one note under each finger number.

4. Play the above. Use LH on the first tetrachord and RH on the second tetrachord.

Since the G MAJOR SCALE contains ONE SHARP (F♯), music written in the KEY OF G MAJOR has a KEY SIGNATURE of ONE SHARP. The sharps or flats in the key signature are indicated at the beginning of the music, just after the clef sign. They remain in effect throughout the music, or until a new signature appears.

5. Complete a tetrachord beginning on each of the notes below. Write one note under each finger number. The sharp in the key signature will apply to the F♯ in the second tetrachord, so you need not write a sharp before the F.

KEY OF G MAJOR
Key Signature: 1 sharp (F♯)

6. Play with RH. Pass 1 under 3.

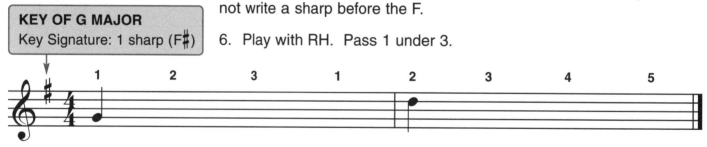

7. Complete a tetrachord beginning on each of the notes below.
   Write one note over each finger number.

8. Play with LH. Cross 3 over 1.

9. Play each of the above two scales in REVERSE, starting with the highest note and descending to the lowest. Play the first with RH, crossing 3 over 1, and the second with LH, passing 1 under 3.

The Primary Chords in G Major

Reviewing the G MAJOR SCALE, LH ascending

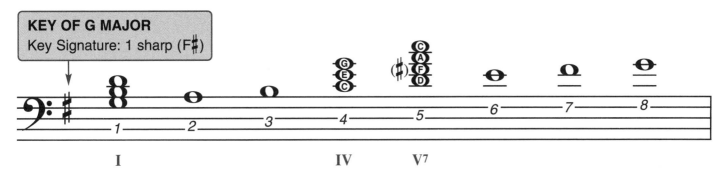

KEY OF G MAJOR
Key Signature: 1 sharp (F#)

The following chord positions
(which you have already learned)
are used for smooth progressions:

Primary Chords in G

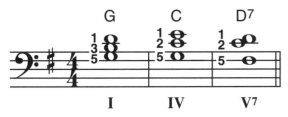

G Major Chord Progression with I, IV & V⁷ Chords

Play several times, saying the chord names
and numerals aloud:

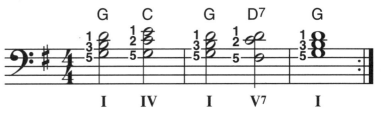

THE MARINES' HYMN 🔊

Moderate march tempo

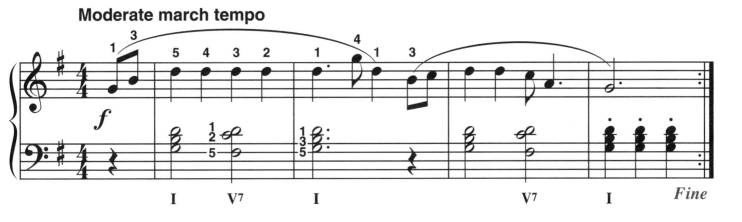

Fine

D. C. al Fine

Notes played between the main beats of the measure and held across the beat are called **SYNCOPATED NOTES.**

WHY AM I BLUE?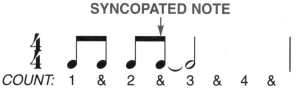

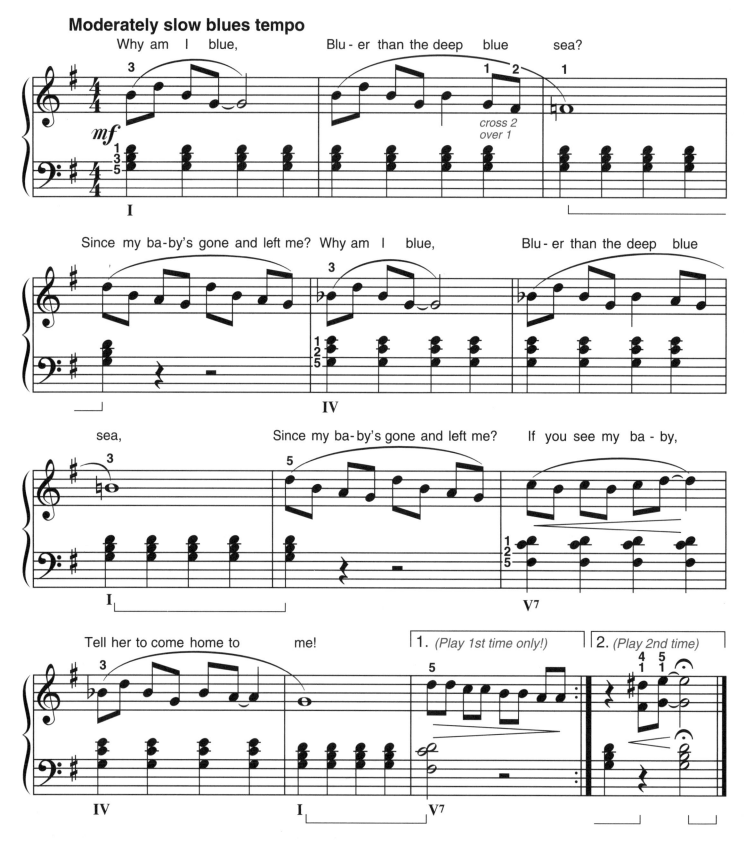

IMPORTANT! Compare the Roman numerals in this piece with those in *GOT THOSE BLUES!* on page 107.

G Blues Scale Performance Piece

GOOD PEOPLE

"Call and Response" is a special technique used in Jazz/Rock to create more excitement.
Measure 9 sounds the call and measure 10 gives the response. Measures 11–12 and 13–14 are used
in the same manner. You may improvise different Blues Scale tones in the "response" measures.

This page is from Alfred's Jazz/Rock Adult Course by Bert Konowitz.

The F Major Scale

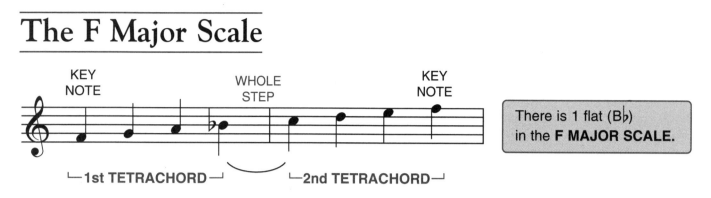

There is 1 flat (B♭) in the **F MAJOR SCALE.**

The fingering for the F MAJOR SCALE with the LH is the same as for all the scales you have studied so far: 5 4 3 2 1 – 3 2 1 ascending; 1 2 3 – 1 2 3 4 5 descending.

Play slowly and carefully!

KEY OF F MAJOR
Key Signature: 1 flat (B♭)

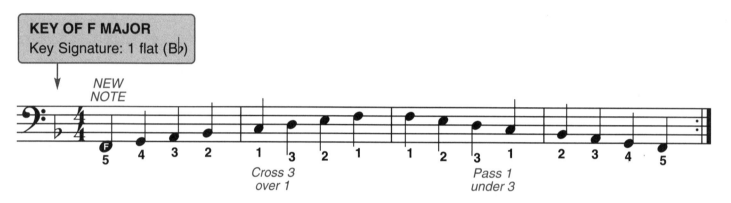

To play the F MAJOR SCALE with the RH, the 5th finger is not used! The fingers fall in the following groups: 1 2 3 4 – 1 2 3 4 ascending; 4 3 2 1 – 4 3 2 1 descending.

Play slowly and carefully!

As soon as you play the thumb, move it under, carrying it at the base of the 3rd and 4th fingers until it is needed. Keep the wrist even, and move the hand smoothly along. Never twist the wrist when the thumb goes under.

Practice the F major scale several times daily. Begin slowly and gradually increase speed.
Play only with HANDS SEPARATE:

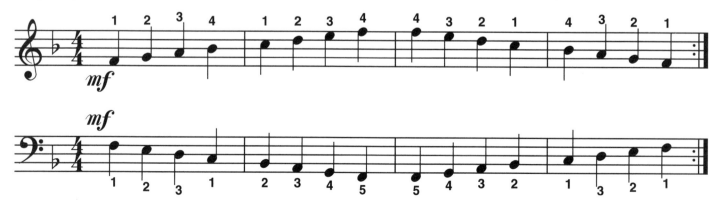

EIGHTH REST means
rest for the value of an eighth note.

ACCENT SIGN means
play with special EMPHASIS!

LITTLE BROWN JUG

American folk song

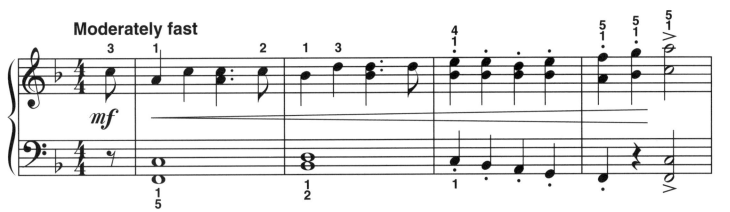

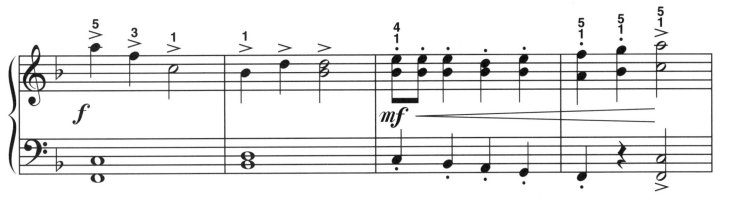

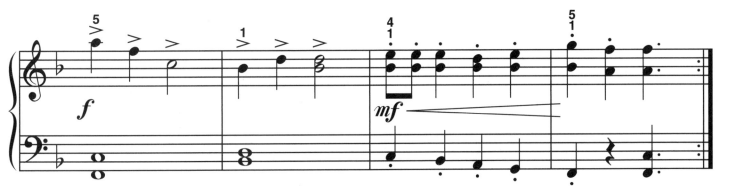

The Primary Chords in F Major

Reviewing the F MAJOR SCALE, LH ascending

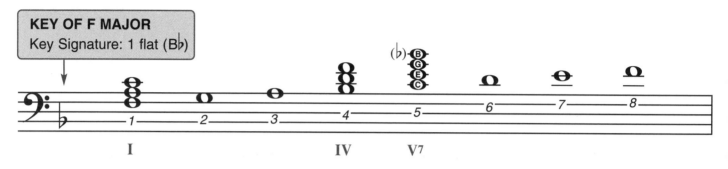

The following chord positions are often used for smooth progressions:

Primary Chords in F

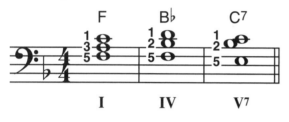

F Major Chord Progression with I, IV & V⁷ Chords

Play several times, saying the chord names and numerals aloud:

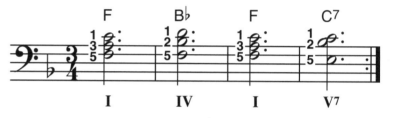

CHIAPANECAS *(Mexican Hand-Clapping Song)* 72

Moderately fast

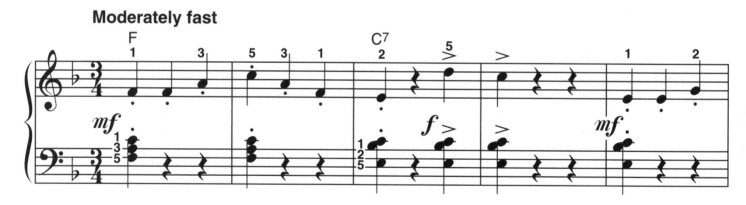

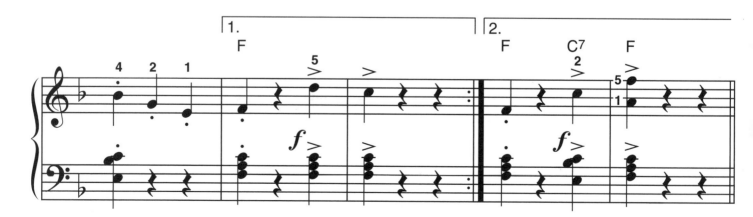

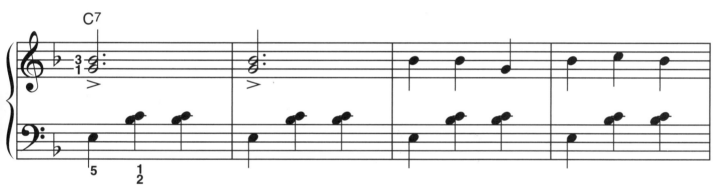

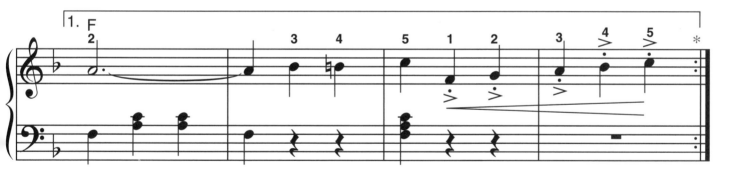

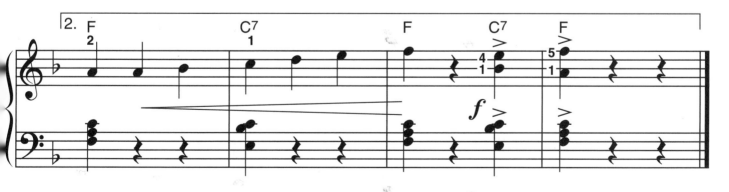

* The double dots inside the double bars indicate that
everything between the double bars must be REPEATED.

Writing in the Key of F Major

1. Write the letter names of the notes of the F MAJOR SCALE on the keyboard below.
   Use the tetrachord patterns, and be sure each whole step and half step is correct!

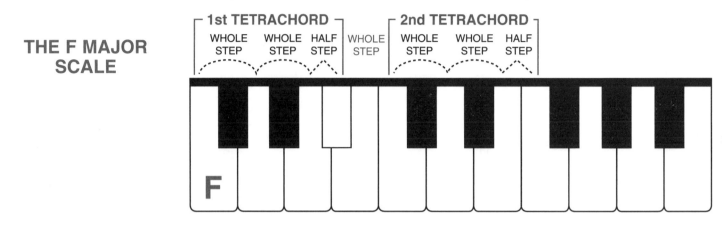

THE F MAJOR SCALE

Check to be sure that you named the notes in the order of the musical alphabet. If you did, the black key will be named as a *flat,* not a *sharp!*

2. Complete the tetrachord beginning on F.
   Write one note over each finger number.

3. Complete the tetrachord beginning on C.
   Write one note under each finger number.

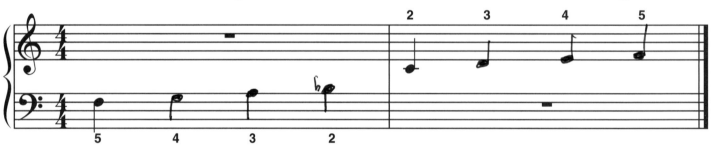

4. Play the above. Use LH on the first tetrachord and RH on the second tetrachord.

> Since the F MAJOR SCALE contains ONE FLAT (B♭), music written in the KEY OF F MAJOR has a KEY SIGNATURE of ONE FLAT.

5. Complete a tetrachord beginning on each of the notes below. Write one note over each finger number. The flat in the key signature will apply to the B♭ in the first tetrachord, so you need not write the flat before the B.

KEY OF F MAJOR
Key Signature: 1 flat (B♭)

6. Play with LH. Cross 3 over 1.

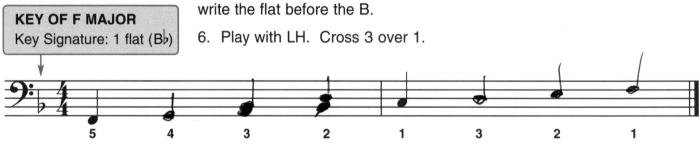

7. Complete a tetrachord beginning on each of the notes below.
   Write one note under each finger number.

8. Play with RH. Pass 1 under 4.

9. Play each of the above two scales in REVERSE, starting with the highest note and descending to the lowest. Play the first with LH, passing 1 under 3, and the second with RH, crossing 4 over 1.

Auld Lang Syne

Old Scottish Air
Words by Robert Burns

A New Style of Bass

Play this several times before beginning *O SOLE MIO:*

Moderately slow

COUNT: 1 & 2 & 3 & 4 &   1 & 2 & 3 & 4 &   1 & 2 & 3 & 4 &   1 & 2 & 3 & 4 &

O SOLE MIO! 🔊

From Enrico Caruso to a recording entitled *In Concert,* by José Carreras, Plácido Domingo and Luciano Pavarotti, this great old favorite has provided tenors with surefire encore material. "There's No Tomorrow," popular in the '50s and '60s, was sung to this melody.

KEY OF F MAJOR
Key Signature: 1 flat (B♭)

Eduardo di Capua

Moderately slow

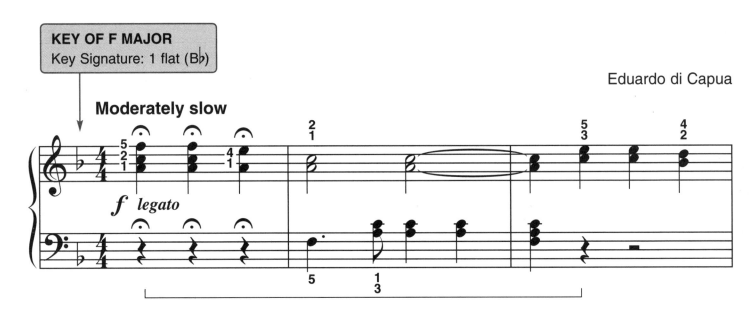

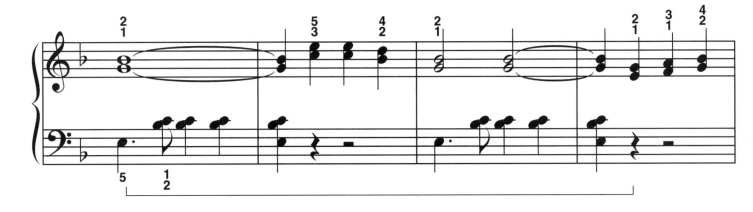

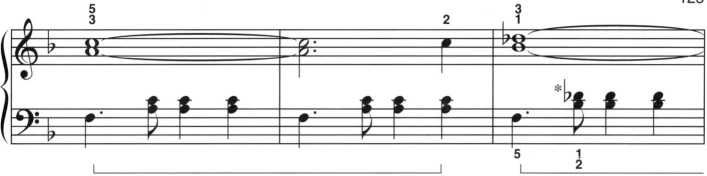

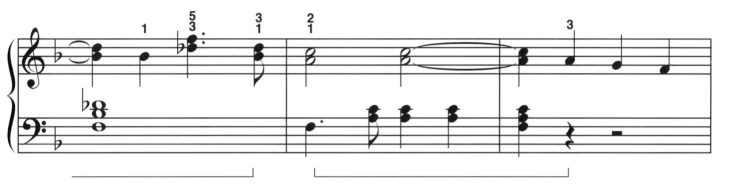

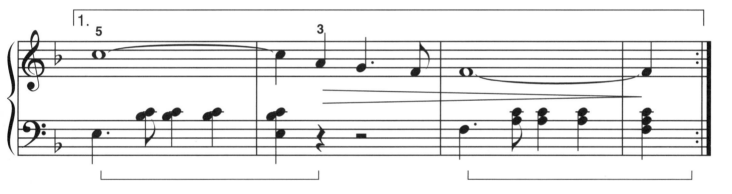

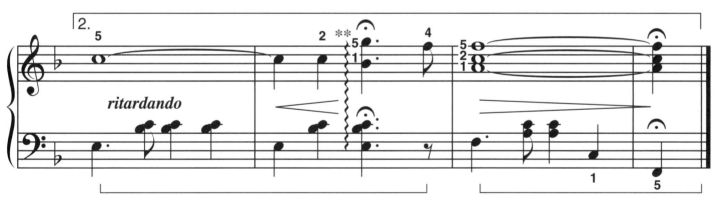

*Note the D♭ in the B♭ chord. This changes the **IV** chord to a MINOR chord, as will be explained later.

**ARPEGGIATED CHORDS

When a wavy line appears beside a chord, the chord is *arpeggiated* (broken or rolled). Play the lowest note first, and quickly add the next higher notes one at a time until the chord is complete. The first note is played on the beat.

The Key of A Minor (Relative of C Major)

Every MAJOR key has a **RELATIVE MINOR** key that has the same KEY SIGNATURE.

The RELATIVE MINOR begins on the **6th** tone of the MAJOR scale.
The RELATIVE MINOR of C MAJOR is, therefore, A MINOR.

C MAJOR SCALE

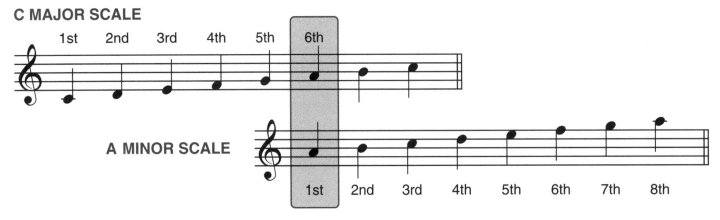

Because the keys of C MAJOR and A MINOR have the same KEY SIGNATURE (no sharps, no flats), they are RELATIVES.

The minor scale shown above is called the **NATURAL MINOR SCALE.**
It uses only notes that are found in the relative major scale.

The A Harmonic Minor Scale

The most frequently used MINOR SCALE is the **HARMONIC MINOR.** In this scale, the 7th tone is raised ascending and descending.

The raised 7th in the key of A MINOR is G♯. It is not included in the key signature, but is written in as an "accidental" sharp each time it occurs.

Practice the A HARMONIC MINOR SCALE with hands separate. Begin slowly.

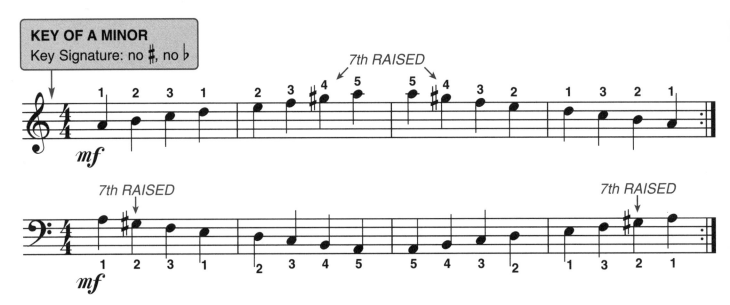

IMPORTANT!   After you have learned the A HARMONIC MINOR SCALE with hands separate, you may play the hands together in CONTRARY MOTION, by combining the two staffs above.

MORE SYNCOPATED NOTES:

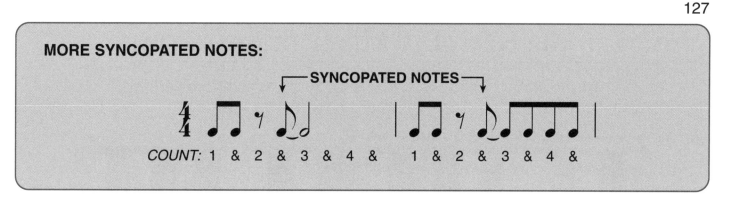

JERICHO 🔊 75

KEY OF A MINOR
Key Signature: no ♯, no ♭*

See how many syncopated notes you can find in *JERICHO*.

Moderately fast

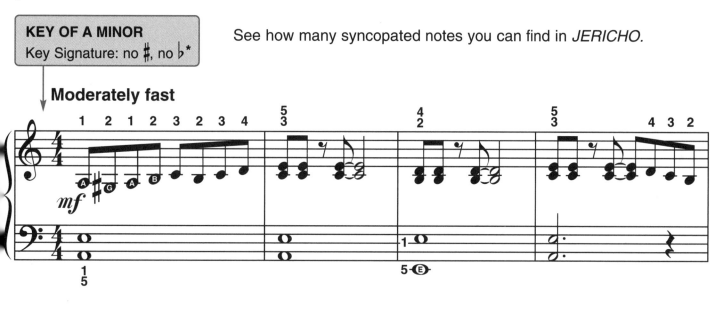

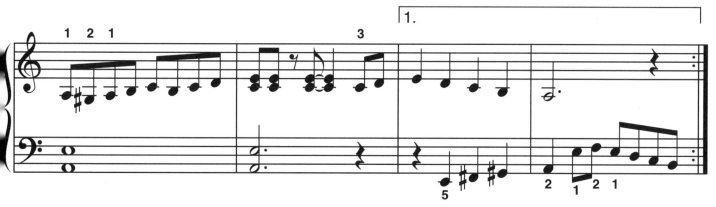

*To determine whether a piece is in a major key or its relative minor, look at the end of the piece. It will end on the key note or chord. This piece has no sharps or flats in the key signature and it ends on A (an A MINOR chord); therefore, the piece is in the key of A MINOR.

Writing in the Key of A Minor (Relative of C Major)

Every MAJOR KEY has a RELATIVE MINOR KEY that has the same KEY SIGNATURE.

The RELATIVE MINOR begins on the 6th TONE of the MAJOR SCALE.

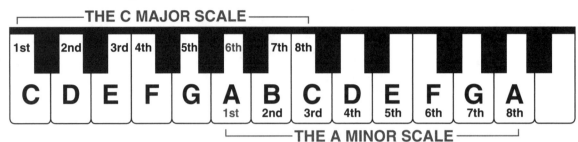

A MINOR is the relative of **C MAJOR.** Both keys have the same key signature (no sharps, no flats).

There are 3 kinds of minor scales: NATURAL, HARMONIC & MELODIC.

THE NATURAL MINOR SCALE: This scale uses *only* the tones of the relative major scale.

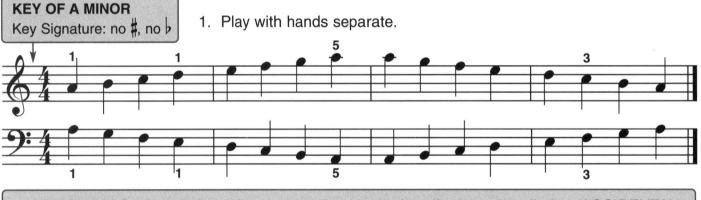

ACCIDENTALS: Any sharp or flat not contained in the key signature is called an ACCIDENTAL.

THE HARMONIC MINOR SCALE: The 7th tone (G) is raised 1 half step,
ASCENDING & DESCENDING.

2. Add accidental sharps needed to change these NATURAL MINOR scales
   into HARMONIC MINOR scales.   3. Play with hands separate.

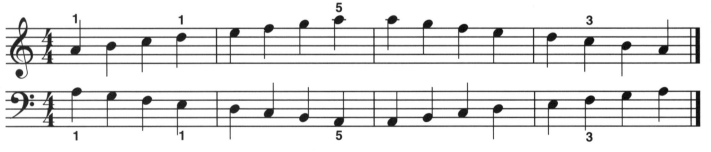

THE MELODIC MINOR SCALE: In the ASCENDING scale, the 6th (F) & 7th (G) are raised 1 half step
The DESCENDING scale is the same as the NATURAL MINOR.

4. Add accidental sharps needed to change these NATURAL MINOR scales
   into MELODIC MINOR scales.   5. Play with hands separate.

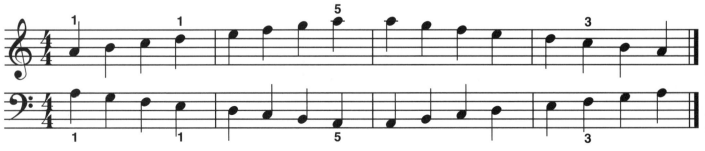

6. (OPTIONAL) Play all of the above scales with hands together, in contrary motion.

An A Minor Chord Progression

THE STRANGER 🔊

This new chord progression includes the A minor chord and is often used in ballad-type Jazz/Rock music. The melody in the RH should be played in a *legato* (smooth) manner while the LH moves down the chord progression at a very steady tempo. First practice measures 1–4 with the LH alone.

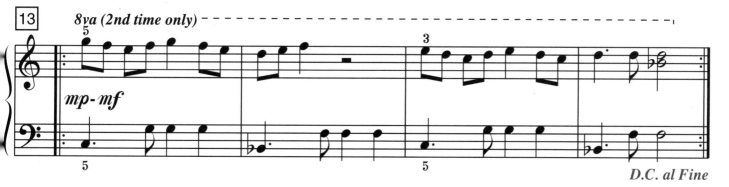

This page is from Alfred's Jazz/Rock Adult Course by Bert Konowitz.

Introducing "Overlapping Pedal"

The following sign is used to indicate OVERLAPPING PEDAL.

PLAY

PED   PED
UP   DOWN

At this point, pedal again.

As the hand goes *down,*
the foot comes *up.*
Pedal again immediately.

Practice the following exercises before playing *GREENSLEEVES.*

GREENSLEEVES

NEW DYNAMIC SIGN

mp (mezzo piano) = medium soft

KEY OF A MINOR
Key Signature: no ♯, no ♭

Moderately slow

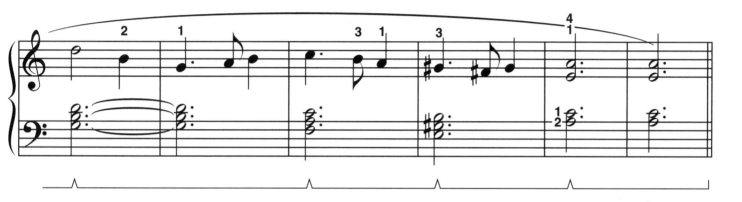

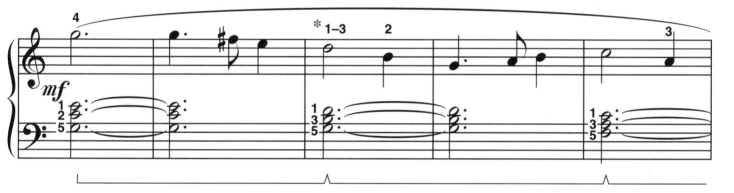

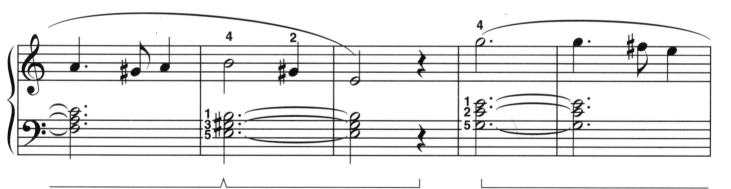

*FINGER SUBSTITUTION: While holding the note down with 1, change to 3 on the 2nd beat.

More About Triads

1. Some of the 3rds you have been playing are MAJOR 3rds, and some are MINOR (smaller) 3rds.

2. All of the 5ths you have played so far are PERFECT 5ths.

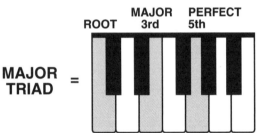

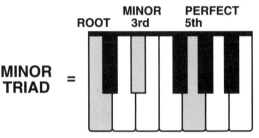

Any MAJOR 3rd may be changed to a MINOR 3rd by lowering the upper note one half step!

3. MAJOR TRIADS consist of a ROOT, MAJOR 3rd & PERFECT 5th.

4. MINOR TRIADS consist of a ROOT, MINOR 3rd & PERFECT 5th.

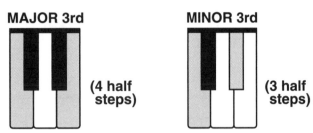

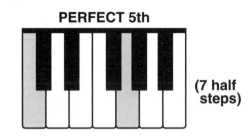

Any MAJOR triad may be changed to a MINOR triad by lowering the 3rd one half step!

5. Play the following triads with RH 1 3 5. Say "C major triad, C minor triad," etc., as you play each pair. Then repeat ONE OCTAVE LOWER, using LH 5 3 1.

The Primary Chords in A Minor

Reviewing the A HARMONIC MINOR SCALE, LH ascending

Small (lower case) Roman numerals are used to indicate minor triads (**i** & **iv**).

Small (lower case) m = minor

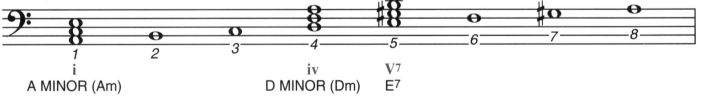

The following positions are often used for smooth progressions:

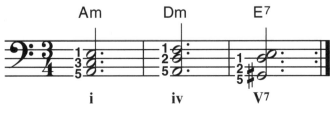

The same, one octave higher.

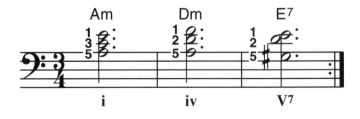

Go Down, Moses

Moderately slow

When Is - rael was in E - gypt's land, Let my peo - ple go! Op -

pressed so hard they could not stand, Let my peo - ple go!

Go down, Mos - es, 'Way down in E - gypt's land,

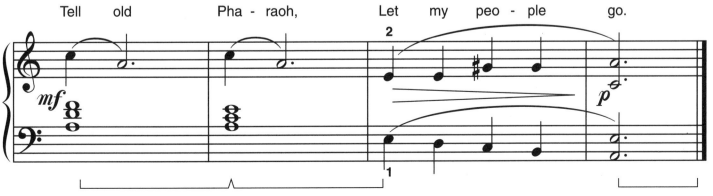

Tell old Pha - raoh, Let my peo - ple go.

The Key of D Minor (Relative of F Major)

D MINOR is the relative of **F MAJOR**.
Both keys have the same key signature (1 flat, B♭).

REMEMBER: The RELATIVE MINOR begins on the **6th** tone of the major scale.
The relative minor of F MAJOR is, therefore, D MINOR.

F MAJOR SCALE

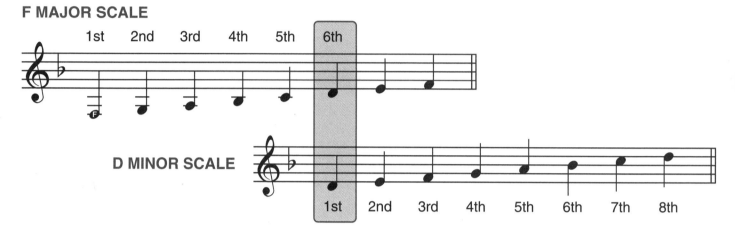

The minor scale shown above is the NATURAL MINOR scale. Remember, the natural minor uses only notes that are found in the relative major scale.

The D Harmonic Minor Scale

In the HARMONIC MINOR scale, the 7th tone is raised ascending and descending.

The raised 7th in the key of D MINOR is C♯. It is not included in the key signature, but is written as an "accidental" sharp each time it occurs.

Practice the D HARMONIC MINOR scale with hands separate. Begin slowly.

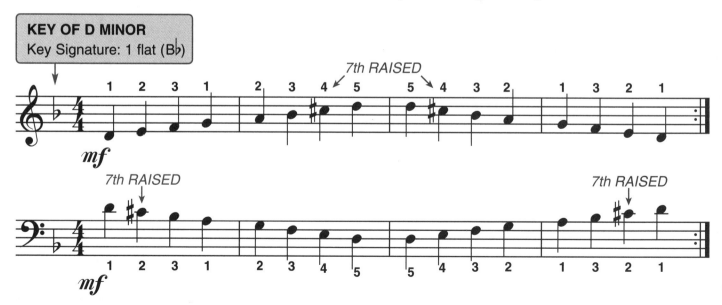

IMPORTANT!   After you have learned the D HARMONIC MINOR SCALE with hands separate, you may play the hands together in CONTRARY MOTION, by combining the two staffs above.

SCARBOROUGH FAIR 🔊 79

NEW DYNAMIC SIGN

pp (pianissimo) = very soft

KEY OF D MINOR
Key Signature: 1 flat (B♭)

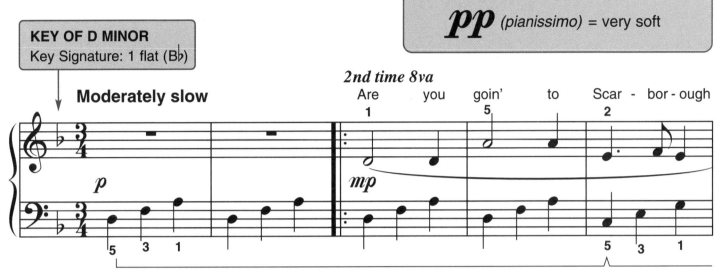

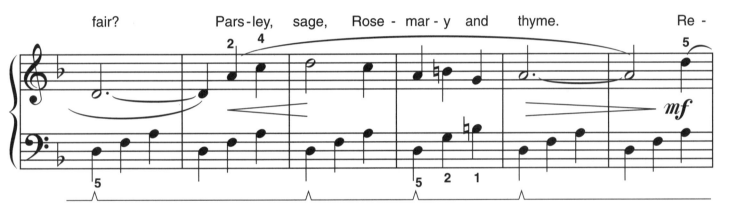

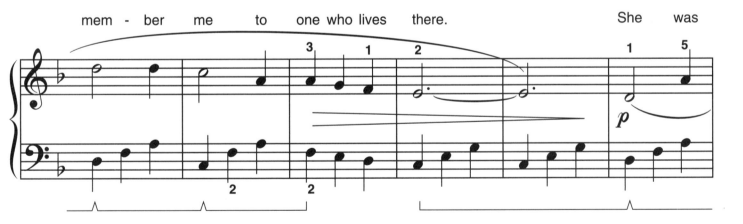

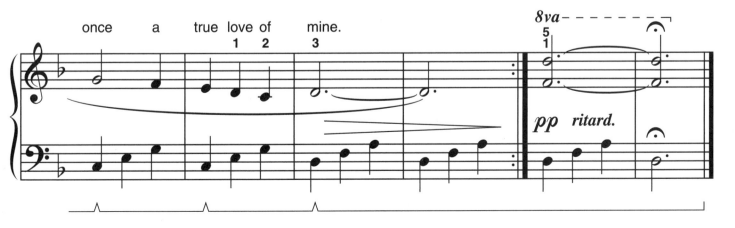

The Primary Chords in D Minor

Reviewing the D HARMONIC MINOR SCALE, LH ascending

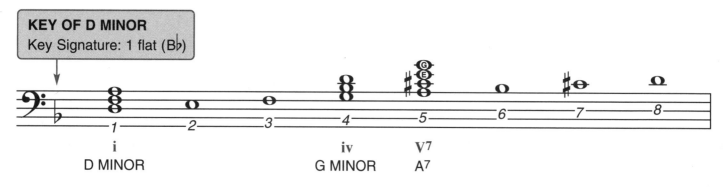

KEY OF D MINOR
Key Signature: 1 flat (B♭)

The following positions are often
used for smooth progressions:

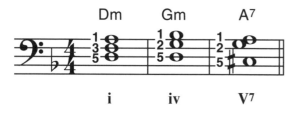

Play several times, saying the chord names
and numerals aloud:

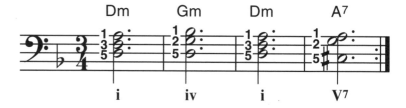

D MINOR PROGRESSION with broken i, iv & V⁷ chords

Play several times.

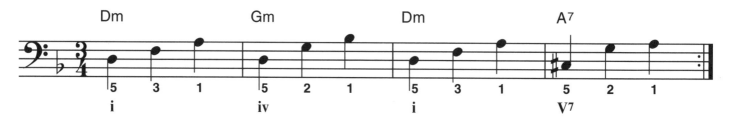

RAISINS AND ALMONDS

Folk song

Moderately

When I was a ti - ny sleep-y - head, Ma - ma

gent - ly would tuck me in - to bed, And

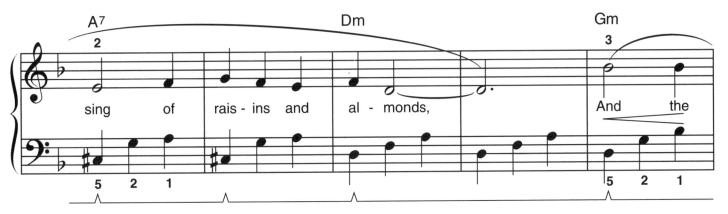

sing of rais - ins and al - monds, And the

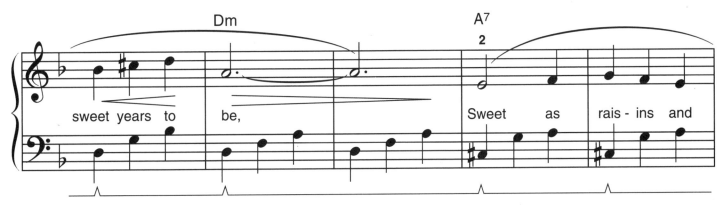

sweet years to be, Sweet as rais - ins and

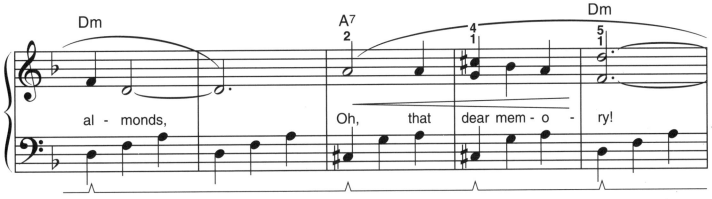

al - monds, Oh, that dear mem - o - ry!

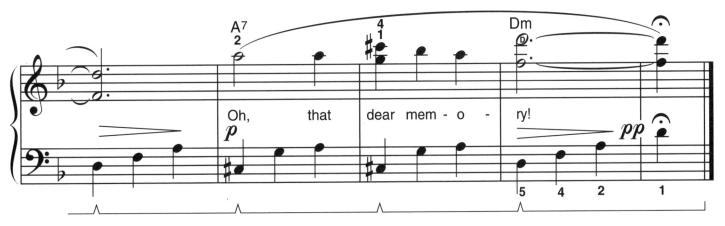

Oh, that dear mem - o - ry!

HE'S GOT THE WHOLE WORLD IN HIS HANDS

This piece reviews the **I**, **IV** & **V⁷** chords of the keys of G MAJOR, C MAJOR and F MAJOR.
It also reviews syncopated notes, in preparation for *THE ENTERTAINER,* on pages 140–141.

KEY OF G MAJOR
Key Signature: 1 sharp (F♯)

Moderately & rhythmically

Spiritual

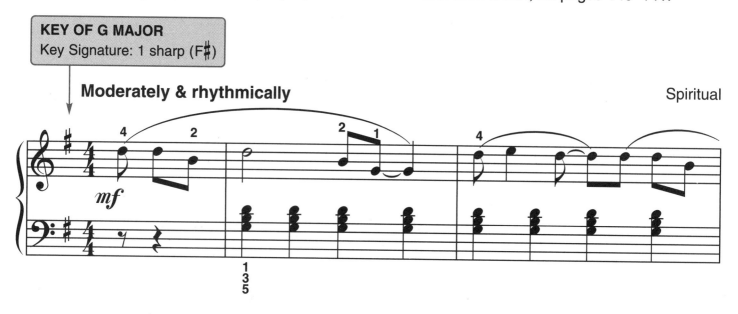

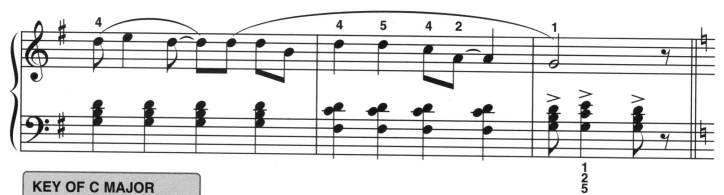

KEY OF C MAJOR
Key Signature: no ♯, no ♭

KEY OF F MAJOR
Key Signature: 1 flat (B♭)

ritardando

(A - men!)

LH Warm-Up

Practice many times, very slowly. These four measures contain everything new
that you will find in the LH of *THE ENTERTAINER!*

THE ENTERTAINER

Not fast!∗

Scott Joplin

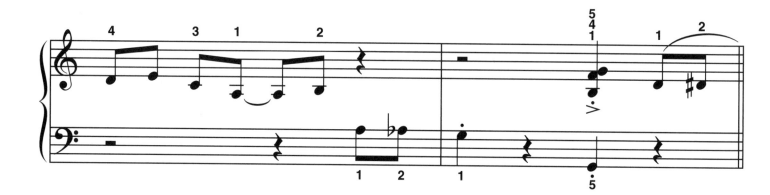

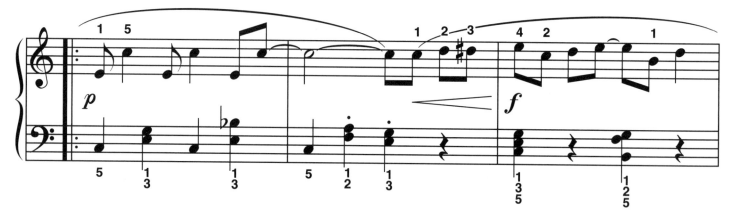

∗ "Not fast" is the composer's own indication!

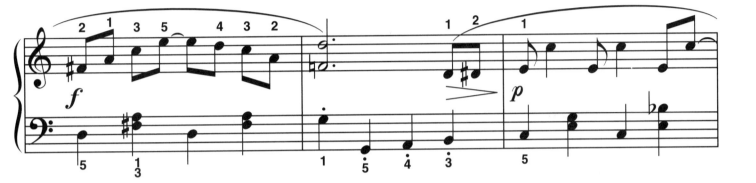

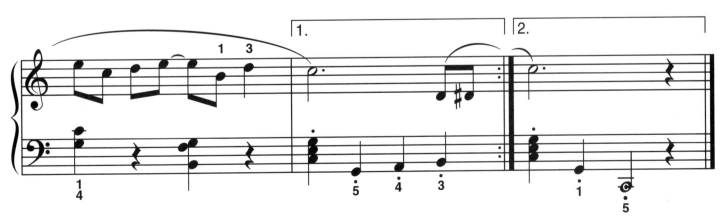

Eighth-Note Triplets

When three notes are grouped together with a figure "*3*" above or below the notes, the group is called a **TRIPLET**.

The three notes of an eighth-note triplet group = one quarter note.

When a piece contains triplets, count **"trip-a-let"**
     or **"one & then"**
     or any way suggested by your teacher.

AMAZING GRACE

John Newton, J. Carrell & D. Clayton
Arr. by P. M. & L.

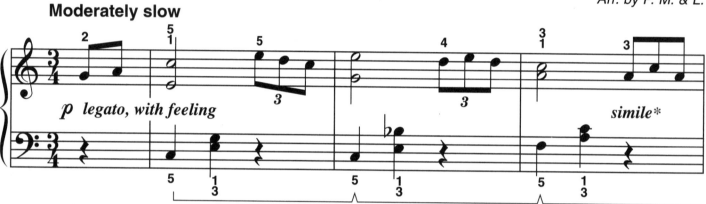

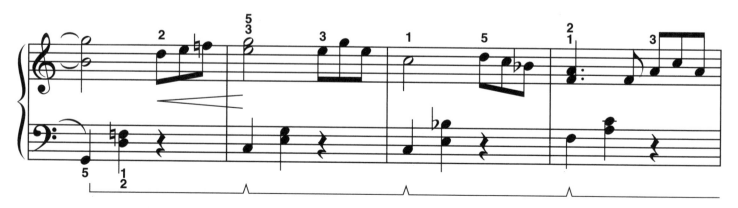

simile = *same.* This means *continue playing in the same manner.* In this case, continue to play triplets each time three eighth notes are joined with one beam.

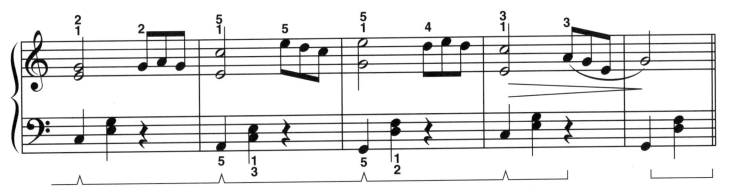

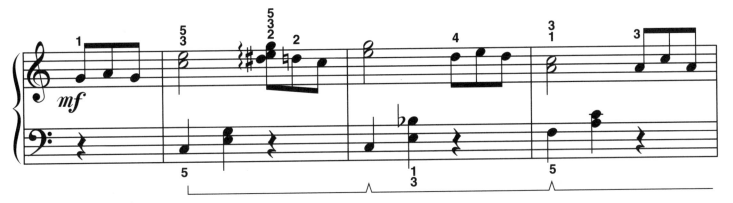

On pages 144 to 159 are seven very popular selections that you have the knowledge and ability to perform.

OVER THE RAINBOW 84

Music by Harold Arlen
Lyrics by E.Y. Harburg

At Last

Music by Harry Warren
Lyrics by Mack Gordon

Slowly, with feeling

* The eighth notes may be played a bit unevenly: long short long short, *etc.*

Singin' in the Rain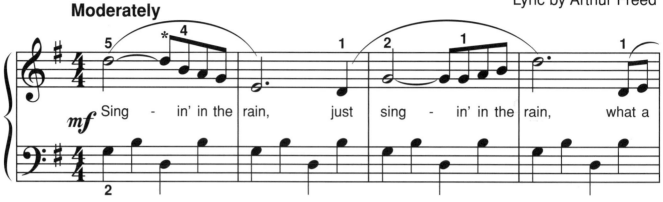

Music by Nacio Herb Brown
Lyric by Arthur Freed

Sing - in' in the rain, just sing - in' in the rain, what a

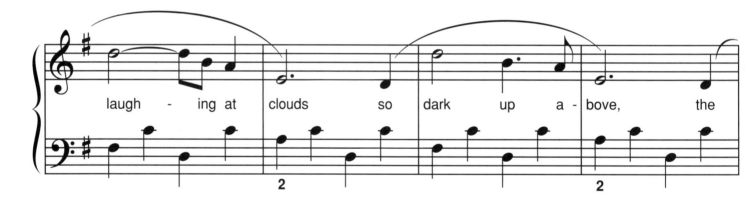

glo - ri - ous feel - ing, I'm hap - py a - gain. I'm

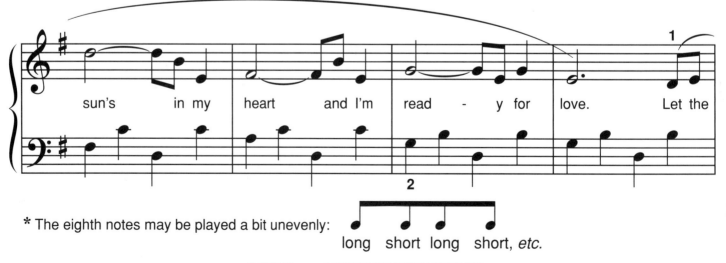

laugh - ing at clouds so dark up a - bove, the

sun's in my heart and I'm read - y for love. Let the

* The eighth notes may be played a bit unevenly:

long short long short, *etc.*

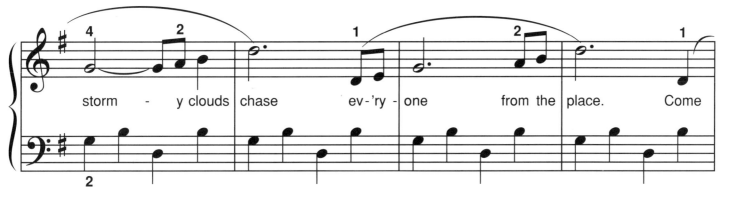

storm - y clouds chase ev-'ry - one from the place. Come

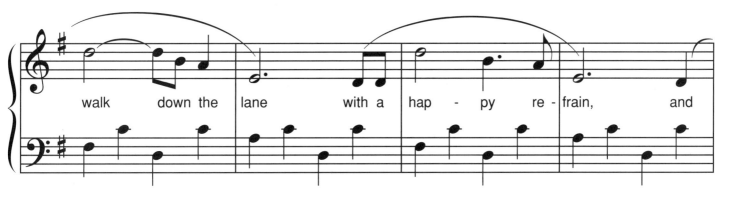

on with the rain, I've a smile on my face. I'll

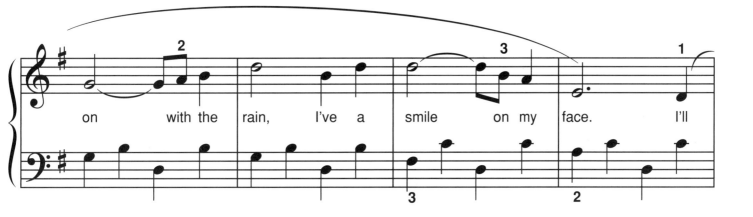

walk down the lane with a hap - py re - frain, and

sing-in', just sing-in' in the rain!

a tempo

ritardando

LAURA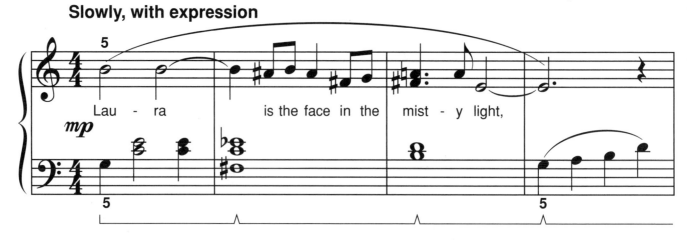

Lyrics by Johnny Mercer
Music by David Raksin

Slowly, with expression

Lau - ra   is the face in the   mist - y light,

foot - steps   that you hear down the   hall,

the laugh   that floats on a   sum - mer night   that you can

nev - er quite   re - call.   And you see

Lau - ra   on the train that is   pass - ing through,

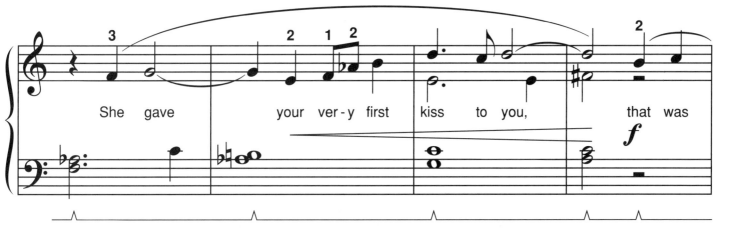

those   eyes   how fa - mil - iar they   seem.

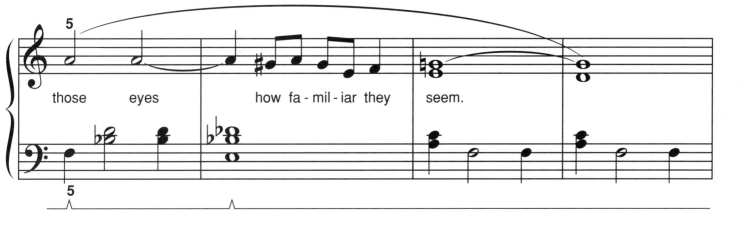

She   gave   your ver - y first   kiss   to   you,   that was

Lau - ra,   but she's on - ly   a   dream.

Have Yourself a
Merry Little Christmas

Words and Music by
Hugh Martin and Ralph Blane

The Ballad of Gilligan's Isle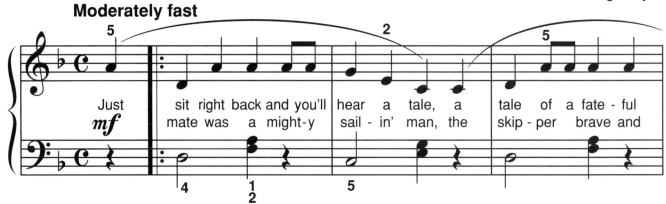

Words and Music by
Sherwood Schwartz and George Wyle

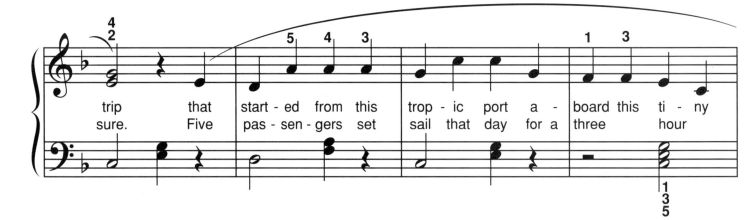

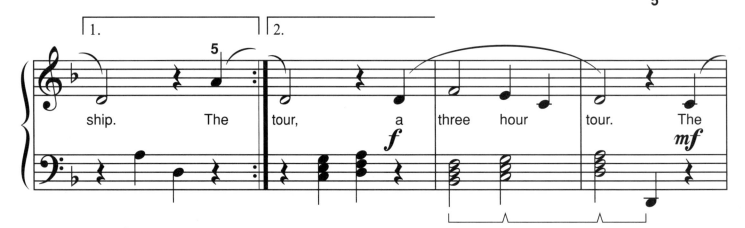

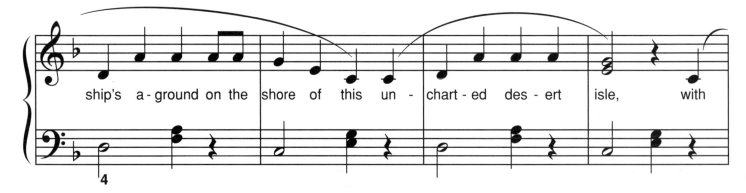

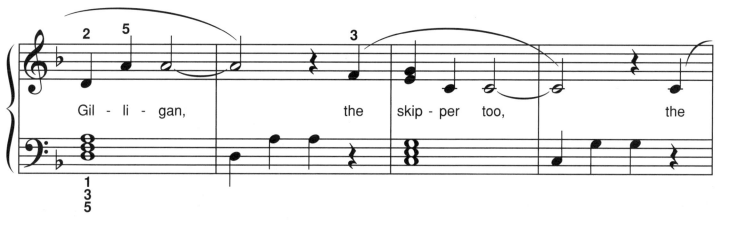

Gil - li - gan,   the   skip - per too,   the

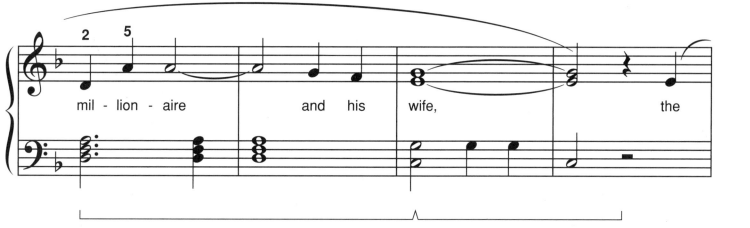

mil - lion - aire   and his   wife,   the

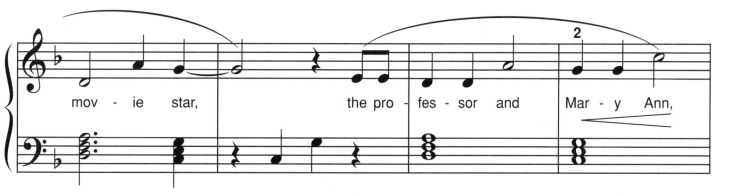

mov - ie star,   the pro - fes - sor and   Mar - y Ann,

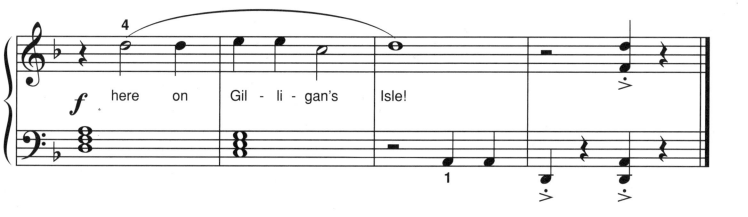

f here on Gil - li - gan's Isle!

CHATTANOOGA CHOO CHOO 🔊

Music by Harry Warren
Lyrics by Mack Gordon

Moderate swing rhythm

Par-don me, sir,
I can af - ford

is that the Chat-ta-noo-ga
to board the Chat-ta-noo-ga

Choo Choo?
Choo Choo.

Track twen-ty - nine,
I've got my fare

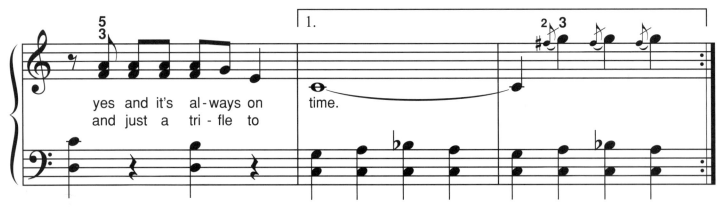

yes and it's al-ways on
and just a tri-fle to

time.

* A short note played quickly before the main note is called a *grace note.*

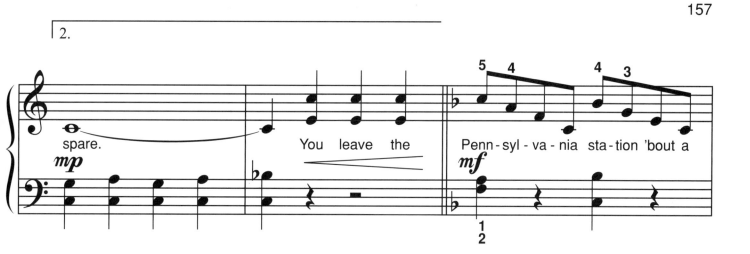

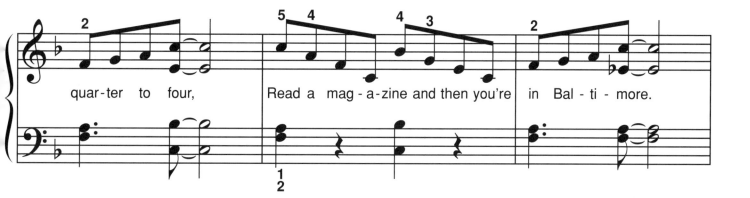

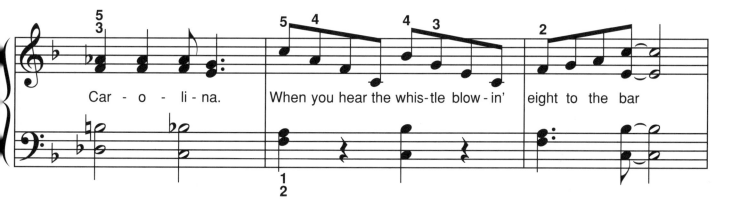

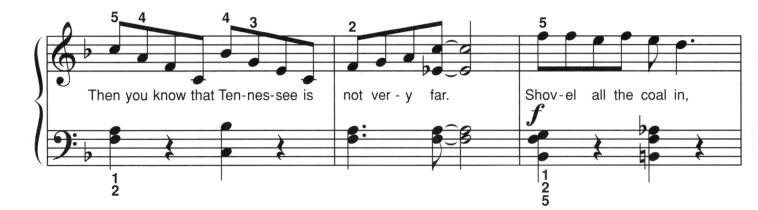

Then you know that Ten-nes-see is not ver - y far. Shov-el all the coal in,

got - ta keep it roll-in'. Woo, woo, Chat-ta-noo-ga, there you are.

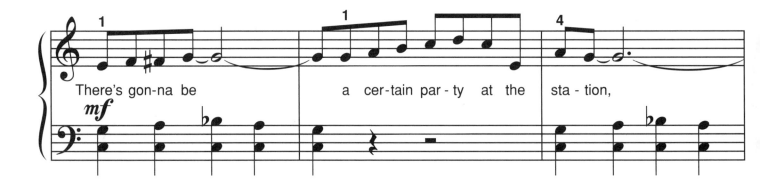

There's gon-na be a cer-tain par - ty at the sta - tion,

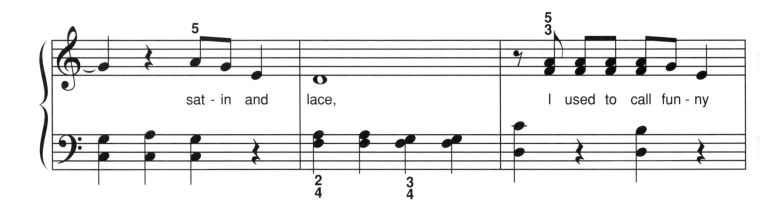

sat - in and lace, I used to call fun - ny

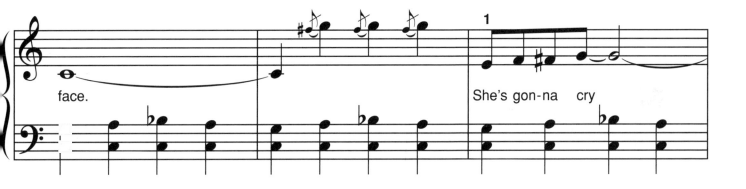

face.   She's gon-na cry

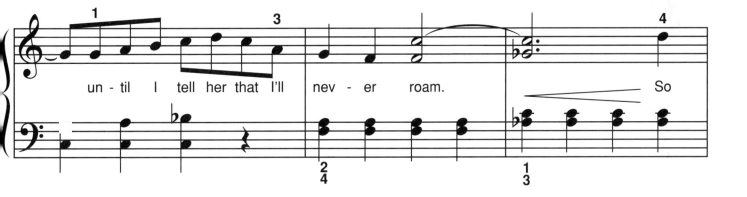

un - til I tell her that I'll nev - er roam. So

Chat - ta - noo - ga Choo Choo, won't you choo choo me home.

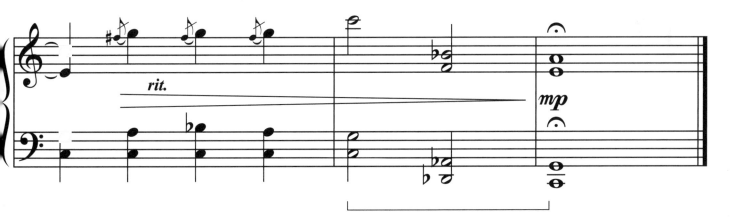

rit.   **mp**

Certificate of Award

This is to certify that

_____

has successfully completed

Alfred's Basic Adult Piano Course, Level 1

and is hereby promoted to

Alfred's Basic Adult Course, Lesson Book 2.

_____   _____
Date   Teacher